<u>Selling Used Dogs</u>

© Robert Cabral 2011
all rights reserved

ISBN # 978-0-9857413-1-0

you can't save all the animals
in the world...

but you can save one...

join the revolution!

www.boundangels.org

Chapters

Your life is short,
but your love is eternal.

You touch me today, and your touch
remains in my heart always.

Foreword

Some of you may take a step back at the title of this book and some may be downright offended. If I've offended you, part of my job has already been done. It's not that I want to offend you, but I want to stir your emotions. Unless we start to look at saving dogs a little differently, and move from emotion to strategy, we will lose this battle, and the casualties are the innocent dogs that look to us through steel bars –sentenced to death for a crime they didn't commit.

If you are a person who says, "We're not selling dogs, we're saving them," well, keep *saving* them and the ones that are left behind still need out, so we may need to *sell* them.

Selling dogs is a two-fold process: One, we need to point out the benefits to potential owners – this is "selling." And, two, we need think outside the box to save more lives. The strategy in these pages will save lives. All of these methods have been tested and proven, with tremendous success.

Remember, these are the animals that the world has turned their backs on for a plethora of reasons. We're left cleaning up a mess that we didn't create. Some dogs have issues and we need to address them. If a dog has a problem, we can either resolve the problem or kill the dog. It's my opinion that we should strive to fix problems and not kill dogs. We need to ask questions to potential adopters and we need to know our "merchandise." I've included my temperament-testing guide in this book to give a better understanding of a dog's personality. As you will see, this guide is not a death sentence for dogs, but instead a guide to better understand what may be ailing a dog and what we can do to help. These dogs should be placed with reputable rescues that can rehabilitate these dogs and place them in suitable homes. *No dog should be killed for a problem that can be fixed.* And most problems can be fixed.

Selling Used Dogs may be an offensive title to some, but I would like to be honest and say that the most offensive thing is what is done to these poor animals every single day.

We have not given up on these animals; we are their only hope. Before you continue reading, sit up straight, take a deep breath and give yourself a pat on the back; you are a hero to these dogs – you are their only hope at life.

This book is also available as a download for anyone in rescue. My goal is to get this information to as many people as possible. I receive hundreds of emails asking for my help, so I found this to be the most beneficial way to help. I ask you not to email your copy of this book, but instead ask your friends, co-workers, rescuers, trainers, etc. to log onto www.boundangels.org and have them download their own copy. I ask for your name and email address so that I can stay in touch with updates. Your email will never be sold or traded.

Thanks for all you do to help save lives!

Robert Cabral

***Please note that there is an inherent risk of serious injury when training dogs and interacting with them. Even the nicest dogs may bite, scratch or attack. I urge you to use extreme caution in all of your interactions.

Starting today we will
Sell Used Dogs and SAVE LIVES…

Join the Revolution!

Introduction

It was a few years back when I visited my first shelter in Nashville Tennessee. It's funny that my first visit to a shelter would be in a city that I lived in for less than two years. This time was a huge transition period of my life. I was working as a photographer at the time and I was so grateful to have my dog Silly, my best friend, healthy and with me as my companion. My life was going well and I wanted give something back. Every week or so I would bring a bag of dog food and drop it at the front desk of the local animal shelter but, as I soon learned, that would never be enough for me.

One day I decided to be brave and see what goes on behind the big steel doors behind the counter. As I cautiously walked to the back, I knew my life would never be the same. I saw beautiful dogs living on cement floors and behind steel bars. Their eyes were empty and their hearts full of despair.

On my next trip, I brought my camera and started photographing them. I had no idea why I was photographing them, but I felt a strong need to do so. I still remember those pictures. The visits went on for the remainder of my weeks in Nashville until I moved back home to Malibu, California.

Once in Malibu I thought I should visit some of the shelters in my home city, Los Angeles. The L.A. shelters were more crowded and not as nice as the shelter I visited in Nashville. I didn't know what I could do, but I knew I had to do something.

The pictures I had taken would come together in a book that I titled BOUND ANGELS. These images would combine my photography and my poetry to form a unique blend of passion and pain. This project immediately told me that my life had to change. I knew what I had to do, even if it was only in my heart. The passion would continue to fuel me every time I wanted to give up.

Lucas was the first dog that I had to save. He was a pit bull / Shar Pei mix. I think the fact that because my Shar Pei – Silly – means so much to me, Lucas would touch me in a way that I can never put into words. He was old, ugly and moved ever so slowly. I could see in the eyes of the employees what the inevitable was, but I would change this.

I immediately reached out to people I had never met. These people would become friends and allies to me over the next several years, and I would pay them back 100 times. I found a sanctuary in Texas that took Lucas and gave him a loving home until his last day. Lucas didn't have long to live – I knew that when I saw him come into the shelter that afternoon. However, I take solace in knowing that my friends Jay and Ricky held Lucas in their arms as he took his last breath. Lucas felt love and died with dignity, something all creatures deserve, but so few ever receive.

I knew that BOUND ANGELS would be more than a book – it would grow to be an organization that would change the way animals are seen and rescued. So many things went into the grounding and development of this organization – including my background in photography, video, design, sales, dog behavior training and just about everything I've ever done.

Please understand that I am writing this book as an animal lover: I've dedicated a large portion of my life to saving animals. The concept of *Selling Used Dogs* is a point-blank way of looking at the problem with no disrespect to the animals we are trying to save. If we can remove a little of the emotional aspect and focus on strategy, it might better help us toward a solution. Although it is difficult for us to remove the

Bound Angels is focused on bringing awareness to the plight of these animals and to educate people as to proper pet custodianship through our sister website www.blackbeltdogtraining.com. However, we are also focused on saving the animals in our nation's shelters.

One important aspect that all rescue organizations, animal shelter and humane organizations can focus on is educating people on proper pet custodianship. This includes, but is not limited to: training dogs and proper care such as medical, pre-screening and relinquishment counseling. The more work we can do to keep one more dog from entering our shelters, the better we make it for these animals – and the more realistically we can focus on getting the animals out of the shelters. If we were to add up the amount of time it takes to rescue, foster and re-home one dog – that time would be better spent in educating people before they dump their pets. It could even be better used by counseling people before they purchase or adopt a dog. One aspect no one wants to address, but I will here, is the psychological damage that happens to an animal when it enters the shelter. Even if the animal did not have an issue when it entered the shelter, it will develop some sort of an issue if it spends only a few days there.

There are those who say a particular dog developed no issues, but I can assure you that these are the most unique cases. How these issues are addressed will mean the difference between a dog that will recover and one that will get worse – and eventually end up back in the shelter, only to become a statistic. How a dog is introduced into a home after rescue is as important as the imprint stage of a puppy, and sometimes more important.

People in rescue often approach rescuing an animal with an open heart and a closed mind. The most heartbreaking dogs get the most attention, while great dogs that are just short of perfect are overlooked and killed. These are the transparent victims of our egos. If the dog has no issues – no reason for us to feel sorry for it – we fix our gaze on the "poor old guy" or the "sweet sick girl" or anything else that captures the fancy of our attention. *If it bleeds it leads* is the old saying in the news, and it's not that different in rescue.

How many times have we seen the email that shows a 12-year-old dog that was surrendered by his owners because they could not afford the medication or the surgery the dog required? The rescue community will rally around this dog and raise thousands of dollars because "he deserves better." If this 12-year-old dog is worth thousands of dollars in fundraising and countless hours of rescue workers' blood sweat and tears so that he may have another year or two of life, irrelevant of quality, ask yourself, "What do you say to the 3-year old dog that has 10 years in front of him?" Does he deserve a life? Does he deserve a chance? Do we kill him to save the other? No one wants to play God, but someone inevitably does in a situation like this.

Yes, every life is precious, and even though we could save 4 or 5 young dogs for the same money raised for the ailing old one, we still stay focused on the one that breaks our hearts. We can't turn away from the sadness of the old dog that was abandoned or is sick, the injured puppy or the deformed stray dog that cries out to us. But I remind you that there is sadness no matter where we turn in this work. I've saved both old, sick dogs as well as perfect pet dogs. They both cry out to me, so I can understand the dilemma.

The only thing that ever brought some clarity to me in this situation was thinking about it strategically. I see the scene in this way: In a shelter, the more that go out the front door, the less will need to go out the back door. In the time it takes to get an older dog out, several younger dogs can be adopted out. *If the effort is put on the more "sellable" dogs, there is a greater chance that the older dog will have a chance to live.* After all, we've created more open kennels, so the older dog should remain safe until we can get him to a rescue. And that is where rescue should come in – saving the dogs that are not adoptable.

In no way am I saying that we should abandon any dog but, given the choice, we should focus on saving the most lives possible. As tough as this is to accept, it's a necessary concept to understand.

I firmly believe that this is where "true rescue" must come in. Perfectly healthy, young dogs that are highly adoptable don't need to be pulled out by rescue on the first day or two they arrive or become available at the shelter. Rescue must remain what it is: **RESCUE**. Dogs that are not in danger of being killed at the shelter are only in danger of adoption.

Some rescue groups paint a bad picture for those who work so hard and are always spending their last dollar to save an animal that is truly in need of rescue. These "problem" rescuers comb the shelters for young, purebred dogs. They "rescue" them and then turn them around, selling them at a high profit. Rescue work for the most part is *non-profit*; it is humanitarian work to help animals that are in the greatest need.

Those doing the hard work of rescue need support, while those that are greedy and work only to benefit themselves need to go away.

Reaching Out

One of the best things that rescue groups, as well as shelters, can do is *"think outside the box."* Often times this means getting dogs to places that will increase their chances of adoption, marketing them differently, with creative campaigns to drive people into the shelters as well as animals out of shelters. This can include adoptions at local parks, malls, outside of pet stores, at events and a host of other places. If the people won't come to the animals, bring the animals to the people.

When reaching out like this, it's best to bring a good variety of pets to create a "sale-ability" factor. If the shelter is overrun with pit bulls or Chihuahuas, don't fall for the hype of bringing all of them to the event in order to sell off what you have too many of. The error in this is that you are cutting out people who may be interested in a lab or a collie or just a good ol' mutt. Also, it's a good idea to shape people's idea of what kind of pets are available at the shelter. Eventually we'd like to see these people come to the shelter, or tell their friends to visit the shelter.

Each animal you get adopted at an event

opens a cage for another animal that will not have to be killed. Be sure that the animals you bring to events are friendly toward people, as well as toward other dogs. Be sure they are clean, and do something cute, like put a bandana around the dog's neck.

**Please see my section on Behavioral Testing for more information on assessing a dog's behavior toward other dogs, people and strange environments.

Our inventory of *"Used Dogs for Sale"* should be the best representation of the shelter; therefore, they should be bathed or at least sprayed with a pet spray and presented in clean kennels. Dressing them in t-shirts and bandanas is always a good idea to make them more *saleable*. A dog wearing a bandana seems to appeal to people more than a dog without one. (I'm not sure why, but people like bandanas and t-shirts on dogs, so just go with it!) Some dogs don't like to wear human clothes, so be aware of which ones will put up with this and which will not. Check with local pet stores to see if they will donate clothes for the dogs. As a trainer, I'm not a fan of dressing up dogs, but to save a life I don't care if we need to dye a dog pink. Also, have plenty of treats on hand so that people can give the dogs treats and create a bond with them. This has a two-fold benefit: first, it makes the dogs more social and accepting of people and two, it creates a relationship and buy-in factor with the people meeting the dog.

The staff at the event should also be very helpful and dressed in a friendly manner. This is a day away from the shelters, so select people who are outgoing and enjoy these types of events. If possible, I would offer an incentive for each dog placed from the event. It doesn't matter if it's two free movie tickets or a certificate of recognition for outstanding service. Getting an employee's buy-in is huge, and employees love recognition. The employees responsible for adopting out pets are the life-line to the solution. If they are not recognized, it's a huge mistake. This includes volunteers as well.

Wherever the event is taking place, make sure that the animals don't get too stressed out and that they have plenty of shade and water. Food will not be as important since they will be getting treats from all the passersby. Let this be a day of *special treats* all day and feed them when they return to the shelter. Feeding dogs at events is generally not a good idea, for several reasons including; the need to relieve themselves after eating, issues with dogs eating around other dogs (territorial issues), flies, etc. The key here is exposure and that is our goal in *Selling Used Dogs*.

At the event have plenty of adoption forms, as well as another sheet to get names, contact info and email addresses.

It's a good idea to have a place for people to express what they are looking for in a pet. *We may not have the right pet for you today, but we certainly would like to contact you when the right one comes along.* These will also be good contacts for networking and donations. Some people / groups will opt to have a donation jar at the event. If you do this, keep an eye on it. Personally I feel that contact information is more important than a one-time donation. Try collecting contact information instead of money; it will pay off more in the long run. Also, have flyers about your organization, bragging about all the good work you do. With these flyers I would include forms for volunteers, as well as an envelope that they can return to you with a donation.

Be certain that your organization is set up as a recognized non-profit organization and state that on the handouts you distribute.

Rescues that Work with Shelters

There are those people who work well as a team and then there are those who are constantly criticizing and doing little except making it harder for everyone. Animal rescue has its share of people that make it bad for everyone. These people constantly criticize and take our focus away from the task at hand. These people are often the ones sending scathing emails, condemning people for doing things "wrong" and stirring the pot. Many good people in rescue "get out" because they can't deal with the negative impact of these nutty few.

These instigators have little to do with legitimate rescue and must be ignored. Too much valuable time and energy is spent on these nut-cases. If I put it to you in simple terms, you will understand: in the amount of time it takes to deal with only one *crisis* from these people, at least 2-4 dogs could be saved. Let them criticize, yell, scream and do what they will – but keep *your* eye on the ball. Truth be told, these people are responsible for the deaths of countless animals because they are taking the focus away from the job at hand. If you have a problem with a shelter, it's not something that needs to be made public. If the shelter is slammed in the public's eye, the public will choose not to frequent that shelter and that means more animals will die. I've had issues with shelters, but I never went public because I knew it would harm those that I am trying to save. The issues I've had have been settled in court and through negotiations.

One of the key things to remember is that shelters and rescue organizations are not enemies. They must work together and put aside their differences. We need each other and developing a close relationship can save more animals than being adversarial. I've had shelter employees and rescue people that I love and those that I hate, but I always put those feelings aside for the greater good of my mission and that is *saving dogs*. Creating a symbiotic relationship is one of the keys to solving the problem, and understanding that we both want to solve this problem is the key to a solution.

Finger pointing has no place in saving animals because more often than not while the fingers are pointing back and forth between rescuers and shelters, they should instead be pointed at the animals we are trying to save. If there is a disagreement, swallow your pride; dust yourself off and save an animal to make up for it. Holding a grudge can cost a life. Put yourself in the animal's shoes for a moment and ask yourself what you should do.

There have been situations in which shelters have killed pets accidentally and a majority of the rescuers are screaming, not realizing that all the screaming will never bring that pet back, and while they are busy yelling about the one that is gone, countless animals are crying, "*Let me out*." Let's direct our focus on these animals. Until the problem is solved, animals will be killed, many needlessly. Let's not overlook the ones we can save. Let's remember the ones that have gone to their deaths needlessly and save the ones we can save as a tribute to the others.

Rescue has a choice when it comes to rescuing: that choice involves working as a team or working as a lone ranger. The shelters are the key to the issue. When shelter workers are frustrated with rescue, they often shut down and become reluctant to work with them. I can't blame them, and probably would feel the same way. I've heard countless stories of rescues calling in to the shelter, yelling that they need a *hold* put on an animal and in the end they never come to pick up that pet. The sadness in this is that inevitably another animal has been killed to make space. Rescues that act in such a manner are the lowest of the low.

Giving hope and then ripping it away is wrong – DEAD wrong.

For those who are upset with these facts, please recognize there is a simple problem –SPACE. If shelters were to keep all of the animals that come in, they would be overrun with pets. There are people in rescue who complain that the shelters kill the pets too soon and then there are those who accuse the shelters of warehousing the pets. Again, as previously stated, there are those who complain about everything, and I would say it's best to cast these people aside and work with those who are similarly focused on a *solution*.

If you are a rescuer pleading to save a life, put yourself in the shelter's situation, if only for a moment. You are one person calling in, but remember there are others asking for the same favor. If the shelter does it for you and the dog that you find so special, why shouldn't he do it for the other person and the dog *they* find special? Each animal is special to someone (I would hope). The key is to save all the ones we can.

<u>*A Picture is Worth*</u>

They say a picture is worth a thousand words and, as a person who has made a pretty good living selling pictures. I can tell you that a picture can also be worth a thousand dollars. Let's take that value and transfer it over to the life of the animal, because what's a thousand words or a thousand dollars compared to the life of an animal?

A good photo is one of the single most important aspects in getting a pet adopted out of a rescue or shelter, yet it is often the most overlooked. The other aspect is the story, and I'll cover that later.

Shelters have little time to spend on getting a good quality picture and therefore blow through this process as quickly as possible, often having to redo it. Getting a good picture of a dog is one of the most difficult things to do (next to getting a good picture of a cat). I've taken thousands of pictures of people, but animals are a totally different story. Dogs move, become distracted and look distorted if you don't get the picture just right. Shelters spend the least amount of time on this aspect, and many times don't even take pictures at all. The sheer number of pets going through the doors of the shelters often makes it unrealistic to spend the time necessary to get a picture, let alone a good one. I suggest, whenever possible, to get a volunteer (hopefully a person with good photographic skills and equipment) to spend a day a week getting great pictures of all adoptable animals and replace the pictures the shelter staff took with the professional pictures.

In order to **sell a used dog** the customer needs a picture and a story. And remember that if the picture isn't interesting enough, they won't read the story. Every shelter should have a camera and someone good at using it. Digital cameras are the only choice because we can see the picture immediately after we take it, and we can take a lot of pictures in a row, and that will greatly improve our odds of getting a good one. The mega-pixels don't matter at this point since we are only using the picture for Internet purposes, and possibly to print a kennel card. Anything above 5 mega-pixels is overkill. The key feature that I suggest in looking for a camera is the speed at which the camera responds to the pressing of the shutter button. Some cameras have a *lag time* and that can cost you the picture. Research which cameras have the best shutter release time and go from there. Get the camera in your hands and see how comfortable it is to use. Small cameras can be dropped too easily, stolen or misplaced. Large cameras are too bulky and break easier. Find a camera that fits easily in your hand and play with it. Take a bunch of pictures; see how fast the camera takes the picture after you push the button. Is the picture in focus?

Tips to getting the best picture possible:

The lighting should be well balanced, not too bright or too dark. Although most things can be adjusted in a photo-editing program, we still want to start out with the best shot possible. Consider an area of the shelter that is outside, if possible, and not in direct sunlight.

The best pictures of dogs are generally taken at the animal's eye level. That means you're going to have to get down to their level. Pictures in which the dog is looking up at the camera from a distance tells me nothing about the dog except that the person taking it had no interest in the dog and the dog has no relationship with the camera. Remember, the camera represents the person looking at the pictures. We take the picture to *sell* the *cute factor* of the dog to those who will look at the picture.

When getting at a dog's eye level, I suggest having someone help you restrain the dog, since dogs will see this posture as a play position and will more than likely charge the camera. It is a good idea to be a little further away from the dog and zoom in rather than being too close.

If you are going to restrain the dog by use of a leash, make sure it's a clean one and not a knotted rope that is frayed. If the dog is tossing and turning and getting tangled up in the leash, the photo will not look good. In rare instances it can be advisable to take the dog's picture through the kennel bars, but I would opt for trying to get a good picture on another day. Oftentimes we can get a better picture of a dog after he's had some exercise, so waiting until after a volunteer walks the dog can be beneficial. Another option is to have someone hold the dog. This can be a great selling factor and show interaction with the dog.

If possible, use two people to take the picture. Remember, it might be twice the staff, but if the goal is to move the animals out the front door, the time and effort spent doing this right will pay off in spades. Most of the time, using two people may actually save time. The second person should stand off camera and work on getting the dog's attention toward the camera. See what drives the dog – a toy, the lure of a treat, or a sound. Whatever it is, the assistant should do *it* while the photographer spends his or her time getting the picture. The photographer should not get involved in trying to get the dog's attention or they will miss a potentially good shot. I often see the person with the camera trying to talk to the dog while another person is doing the same thing. Ultimately the dog doesn't know where to look and the photographer never gets a good picture. The person with the camera has one job – to push the button. Leave the rest of the work up to the helper. It's best to have the helper stand directly behind the photographer or slightly off to the side. You want the dog facing forward with an expressive look again remember to get an eye level shot if it will not put you in danger.

Flashes usually don't look good and, whenever possible, I opt for not using a flash. The flash can distract the dog (especially double flashes), and also make the animal look washed out, since you are relatively close when you are shooting. The best light, hands down, is natural light.

The background should be neutral. Some shelters have opted for building small photo areas. These are a good idea, but there are a few things to bear in mind:

- The background should be a color that does not blend with dogs, so avoid browns, blacks and beiges. Pastels work well and muted colors sponged onto a wall or even a cloth drop cloth can have a nice effect.
- The photo area should be in a spot that has little distractions. Dogs and people walking by constantly will distract the dog and make a good picture nearly impossible. Also, understand that the more the area is used for pictures, the more it will smell like dogs. And, there is nothing that dogs find as interesting as the smell of another dog. Keep the area fresh and occasionally spray it down with some odor neutralizer.

If any volunteers are photographers, get them regularly involved in taking pictures of adoptable pets. Pets photograph best in natural light and during the daytime. These pictures should be taken with a minimally distracting background or the background should be blurred. Professional photographers can achieve this very simply by opening up the aperture on their cameras or using a long lens. Getting good pictures of adoptable pets is, in my opinion, one of the most powerful tools in moving *Used Dogs* out the front door of the shelter.

Another great idea is to have a board of pictures at the entrance of the shelter to show people some of the adoptable dogs when they first enter the shelter. I would advise writing the dog's name on the picture to create more interest in the animal. It's also a good move to put the animal's ID# on the picture so it can be looked up quickly in the computer system. If there is a budget available, it's a nice idea to have large posters of some of the adoptable animals. The price of printing these "posters" has come down considerably in recent years. If these animals get adopted, the posters can be given to the adopting family as a gift or we can make a sticker that says, "ADOPTED" and place this across the picture. Imagine how nice a lobby full of ADOPTED dog posters will look.

I wish, only for one night, that those who dumped you here,

could spend the night on this cement floor instead of you.

If It's Good Enough for Hollywood

Every animal has a story – it's our job to tell it. And, if we don't know the story, it may just be our job to come up with one good enough to get them adopted.

Generally shelters will take some information from the people relinquishing the animal, and that info is public:
- The family moved and couldn't take their 10-year-old dog.
- The dog got sick and they couldn't afford the surgery.
- The owners don't have the time to dedicate to the dog.

The stories are all there. If not, make one up. So you ask, "Isn't that lying?" Well, most movies in Hollywood are make-believe but they spark people's interest enough to make millions of dollars. It's not a lie, it's simply a story that we tell.

If you're going to make up a story, make it a good one. I had a dog that I met at the shelter that had no story; I believe she was a stray. So I took it upon myself to make up a good story about her that got her a home rather quickly. The story was simple, Sandy belonged to George W. and Laura Bush, and when they left the White House the Obamas refused to adopt her and she was dumped at the shelter. Now, this is about as far-fetched as any story I could imagine, but people actually asked if I was serious. I was floored. The video got so much attention on Facebook that there was quite an uproar of people defending and criticizing ol' George W for something he had nothing to do with. All I cared about was that the campaign got attention, and that attention got Sandy a home. A good parody is worth it if it can get some chuckles and save a life.

Another dog I met had a deformed foot that made a V, so I named him Spock from the planet VULCAN. Then there was a small Corgi with German Shepherd colors who became the world's first *Miniature German Shepherd*. The stories go on and on.

Stories can be emotional, funny or shocking – it really doesn't matter. The important thing is to focus on the issue at hand. I have used almost every angle and continue to search for new ones. I keep a little notebook of ideas and when a good one hits me, I write it down and plug it in to some dog somewhere. Remember, it doesn't have to match; it's about a fantasy. The illusion is what makes Hollywood – Hollywood. So if you are going to **Sell Used Dogs**, be creative and go to town.

If the story is true, tell it well. You owe it to the dog to really get his message out there. Half-assing it is not an option. You only have one chance to save this life, and remember – it is a life you are saving. If someone were telling your story to save your life, you would want him to tell it well. I take this mission very seriously, as I never want to lose a life because I half-assed it.

Many times there is no story, so I just talk about the dog.

- Look how nicely Rover takes treats. Just think how easy he'll be to train.

- Look how Sasha likes to get belly-rubs. Can you handle this much love?

- Marley just needs someone to throw a ball for him. Get your tennis racket ready.

- Spot's favorite thing is to chase a Frisbee. Imagine how much fun he'll be at the beach!

When the rest of the world gives up,

I'm ready to get started.

What's in a Name?

As crazy as this may sound, it is true. How often have you seen someone ask the inevitable question, "So, what's her name?" The response can bring out a variety of emotions, and how they relate to the dog can make or break it for the dog. In the case of dogs that we are trying to adopt out in pairs, this is even more important. There was a pair of Chinese Shar Pei in a local shelter for over a month and their time was running short. No one was paying attention to them despite of what I thought was a great story. The female was blind and her "boyfriend" was not. I went in and met them and immediately renamed them ***Romeo & Juliet***. I shot a video and put it on YouTube and it was an immediate hit. Everyone was able to identify with it, and these people rallied to raise the funds to save these two beautiful dogs. To me it was quite simple. If you'd like to see the happy rescue of "Romeo and Juliet," check the Bound Angels YouTube channel.

There's also the story of the two cats that were speckled black and white, I called them O and Reo. Now, who would adopt O and leave Reo behind? No one. They were both adopted. There are many options available – here are a few:

Abbott and Costello
Frick and Frack
Bonnie and Clyde
Thelma and Louise
Manny, Moe and Jack
Jack and Jill
Bud and Lou
Batman & Robin

When it comes to individual animals, I try to make the name evoke some sort of emotion from the viewer. On two different occasions I had a dog that was a little overweight and a bit older. They each had been totally overlooked for a long time at the shelter and on both occasions I used the "LARGE MARGE" name to great success. Dogs should be named in a way to reflect their age, personality or characteristics. Naming an old Labrador Brittany doesn't make as much sense as naming her Gladys. Dogs can be named after movie stars, music stars or celebrities. I've seen rescue organizations find great success in using first and last names such as Brad Pitt, Lady Gaga, Clint Eastwood, etc. I personally have used this to a lesser degree, but would suggest trying it. The key point to remember is that the name should somewhat match the dog or evoke an emotion, and it should be unique. Here are some names that worked incredibly well in their specific cases:

Lola
Charlie Chan the Chinese Shar Pei
Sandy Bush (George Bush's dog)
Jesse James
Spencer Tracy
Rico Swavee
Ethel
Godiva
Beso
Bella
Valentino
Pomegranate
Spock
Ludachris
Jerry Springer
Zeus
Dilly
Dolly
Ozzy

… and the list goes one and on. Take a look at the Bound Angels YouTube Channel for all of the creative names that have saved dogs.

For those that criticize this, please understand that I'm showing you a system that works. You've got to make this dog as interesting as possible. Think of the used car salesman in the loud shirt. There are 200 dogs at your shelter and you have to move them because more are coming in every day. A few creative sales techniques will allow you to save more animals than sticking to a system that isn't working.

Selling Used Dogs is about being creative, being edgy and saving lives. I can assure you, no dog is going to complain that he doesn't like his new name. Just ask Ozzie the Prince of *Barkness*. I gave him that name because he reminded me of Ozzie Osborne. He was due to be killed at the shelter because he was old, aggressive and a breed that there were too many of. He was showcased on the Bound Angels YouTube Channel, rescued within a few days and then eventually adopted into a loving home because of the creativity of the Prince of *Barkness* video.

Shelter Angel Videos
Lights - Camera - Action

Perhaps one of the most uniquely successful ideas ever introduced into rescue is the Bound Angels Shelter Angel Video Program. I stumbled upon the idea quite by accident. I wanted to have a tool to better remember the dogs I was seeing at the shelter, and since I tend to have a weak memory at times, I thought this would help me. Also, I would be asked occasionally to evaluate the temperament of a dog; generally to prove it was a good dog – that it wasn't a biter, that it could get along well with other dogs, etc. One day I thought it would be funny to make a story around the dog and the idea was born.

I can tell you that the success rate we've seen with these videos is unbelievable. People love the idea because each one is different and each one makes a star out of the dog (or cat) in the movie.

Since introducing the idea, I've been able to get Los Angeles Animal Services to get on board and even create a special link on their site for our videos. Several volunteers have followed suit and added the videos to their shelters, some good, some not so good. My idea is that everyone can copy my format,

43

and if it is copied exactly – it works. Those that simply march the dog in front of a video camera and state the dogs name, age, breed and ID# are not making a video. These videos do little to showcase the animal, and often times this dog would be better served with a good quality still picture instead of a video.

The inherent flaw with the video program is that it requires two special skills to make the video work. The first one is someone who is dog savvy and presents themselves and the dog well on camera. This person should not steal the show, but also should not be trumped by the dog. It is *this* person who will show all of the good qualities of the dog and make the viewer "see" him or herself with the dog: this person is our **Used Dog Salesperson**. I never thought I had a gift for this until my friends Ken and Liz pointed it out to me. I only did it because I didn't have anyone else I could drag down to the shelter with me on a regular basis. I had the camera and I knew my schedule. I think the most important thing in this person is that they must be able to read the dog. Some dogs are fearful, dominant, show-offs and a host of other things – the person must be able to make the most of the individual characteristic of the dog and bring out his true personality. This person should not

44

constantly pet the dog or let the dog lick their face – this is not selling a dog, it's taking up time. I don't care if the dog licks your face, and many people don't want a dog that licks their face. I want to see the dog move, run, sit, take treats, interact with people as well as other dogs, etc. The key thing is the sale-ability of the dog. Why would someone want to take this dog into his or her lives for the next 10 years? If all I see in your video is you sitting with the dog and he is doing nothing but crawling on your lap, and I hear dogs barking in the background as you are telling me, *"**Rover is so sweet. He just loves people and dogs…**"* Blah, blah, blah… *Sell me the damn dog*! Show me… a picture is worth a thousand words – and a video is worth a dog's life. My goal is to make videos that people want to watch even if they aren't interested in adopting a dog. My videos entertain me, and if they entertain me, I know they'll entertain someone else.

The second required skill is someone to shoot and edit the video. Often times the same person can shoot and edit the video. The key I've found is coming up with a great story, which is what sells the dog. Shooting the video I think is the easier of the two parts. I generally hand the camera (already running) to the person with me, usually a shelter employee. I then get in front of the camera with the dog, a toy, some treats and go to town selling the dog – or letting the dog sell himself, as is often the case. Just my interaction will usually bring about something that I can use later in editing. Whatever the dog is doing that I find interesting is what I will focus on highlighting and bring out. Dogs that stand up on their back legs for a treat, dogs that will sit and lay down, dogs that will chase a ball – there are a million other things. The key is to find something (and all dogs will do something) and make it entertaining.

So many funny videos come to mind that received so much attention and eventually got the dogs saved. I think of myself when I create the stories, and ask the inevitable question, "Would I spend 2-3 minutes watching this video?" and "Is it compelling enough to get someone to want to save this dog?" If the answer is yes, then I know it will be a good video.

The story is generally developed after the video is shot; as I watch it later, something usually comes together. Setting out to shoot a video with a preconceived story is nearly impossible because a dog will not do what you want it to do in an environment like a shelter. You're better off to let the dog have fun, run 10 minutes of video and then piece something together in the editing session.

Editing is so simple these days with the advent of iMovie and a host of other free video editing programs and laptop computers. I use professional editing software to make my movies, but it would be just as well with simple free editing software (I just can't figure out how to use them).

It's paramount to put some kind of music underneath your video. I've found that the music somehow pulls in the audience in a way that I can't explain. People always say, "Your music is so perfect for the story." I have never put too much thought into that aspect of it. I listen to a few loops and try to figure out what "seems" to match. Most of the time I'll start out with a few clips of the dog and then find a loop, lay it under the video and run my editing session based on the song / jingle. Certain editors put the music in last. See what works best for you, but remember music is a key element.

There is nothing worse than watching a video of a dog at a shelter with the cries of hundreds of other dogs in the background. It's not only depressing – it's downright disturbing and distracting. Cut the sound of the shelter 100% and add some music. Some people use commercial songs over their videos (something I rarely do). Sites like YouTube have recently been allowing this, provided that an ad for the sale of the song rides beneath your video. If you're okay with that, cool. Sometimes a commercial song can be very beneficial.

I urge you to watch some of the videos that I've produced on YouTube and get an idea.

Check out: www.youtube.com/boundangels
or get the link directly from
www.boundangels.org

How To

Shooting these videos is quite simple. There are only a few things that people want to see in a video:

- Will this dog fit into my life?
- How is he with other dogs?
- What does he look like?
- How much work will it take to integrate him into our lives?
- How do I get him?

I address each of these issues in a fun, interesting way. Since no dog is perfect for every person, I push whatever trait the dog shows most strongly and make that the focus of the video. For example, if I find a dog that loves treats and will do tricks for a treat, I emphasize that this dog will be easy to train and impress your friends with. If the dog won't do anything for me (treat or no treat) I stress that the dog is very low energy and would be the perfect dog to just hang out with. If the dog is high energy then I focus on the benefit of a dog like this to get you into shape. See what I'm getting at?

How a dog relates to other dogs is usually one of the biggest issues for people in considering adopting a potential dog. People generally don't want to adopt a dog that is

49

dog-aggressive, let alone handler- or people-aggressive. This is something that should be worked out and disclosed in fairness to everyone concerned. Dogs with dominance or aggression issues should be placed with rescue organizations capable of retraining such a dog. As a behaviorist, I firmly believe that most dogs can get along with other dogs – providing the introduction is handled properly. The problem is that most people NEVER handle this part properly. If a dog is friendly with other dogs, I stress that. If he's shy, I focus on the fact that he needs socialization and that he would be a good *only friend* to you (the viewer).

I do try to show a dog with another dog whenever possible, and I stress that shelters and rescue organizations focus on this because people will inevitably run into other dogs in their daily lives, even if this may be *their only personal dog.*

One of the biggest issues facing dog owners is a dog that is dog-aggressive. Well-trained / socialized dogs are rarely dog-aggressive. (I will stress this later in this book.) It is very important for shelters and rescue organizations to do some work to prevent dogs from developing behavioral problems such as dog-aggression. This can be done relatively simply by keeping dogs socialized

– for example taking them for walks together, play sessions and keeping dogs together, preferably two to a kennel.

Looks are everything to some people, so play it up. Like a used car, a *Used Dog* has to fit into the vanity of the person *buying*. The video should have lots of close-ups of the dog: especially eyes and particular markings. I like to use slow motion shots (something that can be added while editing) in order to capture a particular look. Some dogs look better from the side, from the front, running, sitting, etc. Use whatever sales tool you need to get the best representation of the dog. The dog doesn't have to be beautiful – beauty is different to each person.

If you're *selling a used dog*, you've got to make the dog available. That means put a website address, phone number or email address into the video, along with the dog's name. Also tag all of the info about the dog: name, age, fixed, and where and when he / she is available. The information should be available in the video itself as well as on the site where the video plays (i.e., YouTube and the emails that you are sending out).

The overall format of my videos follows this simple pattern:

- Intro: *Hi, I'm Charlie and I need someone to love.* Keep it short!
- Personality traits: *I really love treats, look how gently I take them.* You're selling the dog. Don't lose sight of that.
- Other dogs: *I don't get to be with other dogs much, but look how happy I am when I do get to play.*
- The pitch: *If you adopt me, I'll love you forever.* This can be funny, sad, and / or anything emotional.
- The info: *To adopt Charlie, please visit the Smithtown Humane Society located at 124 Main Street, Smithtown, CA.*
- The animal's ID# and info: *Charlie is a 3- year-old lab mix, neutered and up to date on all shots. He weighs 60 lbs. and his ID# is A1234455.*

All of this info is printed on a ***black card*** with easy to read fonts such as ARIAL, TIMES NEW ROMAN, etc. Don't get too fancy or you'll lose the sale. Your job is to keep the video clean and to the point – it's the dog you're selling, not your video skills. Eliminate fancy transitions and effects. Keep it simple and keep the focus on the dog. The best videos are the ones that people get lost in, not those they comment on with things like, "Wow, I love the great transition and fades you used". If your video saves a dog's life, it's brilliant, if you're too involved with the technical side, consider a career in wedding video production.

The music I use for my videos is generally something that can be downloaded – or purchased over the Internet. They are called royalty-free loops. These are soundtracks that can be bought and placed under a movie and repeated or looped if they are too short. Sometimes editing software will come with a package of loops and more can always be added. The reason I opt for this over someone talking / narrating is that the talking puts another element into the video that can *sway the sale*. I used to speak in my videos, but noticed that the sound was terrible because the environment was not conducive to filming. Also, I found that people tend to get caught up in what I'm saying or what's going on – some people could not divide their attention properly. Take a look at some of my older videos and you'll see what I mean.

That is why I've gone to the black card idea. Simply inserting a black title card with some simple white text written on it is the easiest way for people to get the story. It's also very practical, in that people can pause the video and write down the info. This is not possible if you're speaking the information.

The story should be short and each title card should only have one or two sentences on it. Long stories have to be broken down into the most interesting facts that move the story along. Once you get your story laid out, sit back and watch the movie a few times. When you get to the cards that need to be read, *READ THEM*. But read *EACH AND EVERY WORD*, not the sentence that you wrote, and don't pause the video. Because you wrote it, you know what it says, so you'll tend to blow through it. I read each word - - *ONE by ONE*. If I need to add more time, I will stretch the title card to the time necessary to read it. The general rule-of thumb is that it takes 3-4 seconds to read a sentence or two on the title card. Do NOT make the mistake of having people rush to read the info. I never put more than two title cards back-to-back, unless it is for an effect. The words need to mesh with the video to keep the people focused on what they are buying, which is the dog. I've found that it's better to give the cards an extra second of breathing room rather than rushing through them.

I've also found that the sounds of the shelter

can be a turnoff to people watching. Although I've used this tool to evoke emotion, I want that to be on my terms. If I want people to feel empathy, I can do that much easier by the use of a sentence or a picture or some music. The barking and disarray of the shelter, more often than not, will only add confusion to the person watching. I want them to pay attention to my message – *my sales pitch.*

The best videos that I've produced are about 2:00 minutes in length, never longer than 3:30 minutes. We are dealing with the *Internet generation* – it's all **got to get said in 3 minutes or less.** If the video is too short, people don't feel it's important enough; if it's too long they lose interest. The key to timing these videos is that they work at the 2:00 - 3:00 minute length – with the rare exceptional video of 1:30 minutes. It's been tested and proven – don't try to re-invent the wheel!

Shooting in HD is the best option and really the only way these videos should be done. Most point and shoot digital cameras (as well as some cell phones) will shoot HD 720p video. All-in-one camcorders like the FLIP Video are also a good, low-cost option. Any newer computer will be able to edit in HD and I believe the quality of uploading a HD video to a video broadcasting site such as YouTube will render a better quality video and will better *sell your dog*. Remember, it's a visual element – make it look good.

Whoever is filming the video has to keep a couple of things in mind:

Hold the camera as still as possible. Don't move all over and don't zoom in and out. If you need to use a tripod, do so. I don't use one because the video becomes *too* static, I want some movement, but the video should not look like it was shot on horseback. Remember, we are shooting video, not stills. There is a big difference. The camera should be held still for short periods of time to establish a shot.

Get close-ups of the dog doing some interesting stuff, and always be ready. The minute you're not paying attention is when the best stuff happens. A great example of this is a dog licking the lens of the camera or nuzzling the camera with his nose. This is one of the cutest things I can imagine, and it works great as a transition from one scene to another.

Get wide shots of the environment. A dog running into frame, or playing with another dog is always nice to see. It also gives people a good indication of the dog's energy level.

I try, and suggest you try, to *get a quick video of the dog inside of his kennel*. If the dog can live in a kennel that small, people will understand that the dog *can* live in an apartment if it gets a walk or two a day. Shooting a few seconds of the dog in his kennel oftentimes evokes an emotion in people that reminds them that the dog *is* living in a cage and needs their help. Don't get in the habit of doing this too regularly, as it can become a bit redundant.

Get some video of the dog taking treats or playing with a toy. SELL SELL SELL! These interaction shots between the person *selling the dog* and the dog gives people a buy-in factor and an emotional hook.

All interaction is good. Stay low and keep the camera rolling. You can edit out the trash later. Sometimes the stuff you think won't work while you're shooting makes the best footage. I generally aim to shoot 10-15 minutes of video that I can then edit down later. Considering the addition of the black cards, shelter and dog info, you will still need 2:00 minutes of good footage. This can be trickier than you think, so shoot enough.

Make sure that the video is shot in normal conditions as far as light goes. Since "normal" is such a unique concept for everyone, let me clarify:

Don't shoot in direct sunlight. This is to say, don't overexpose the scene. A sunny day is okay, but keep in mind where the sun is and don't shoot directly into it. If you do, your subject (the dog) will be terribly underexposed. Many cameras do have a setting for *backlight* – if necessary, use it.

Don't shoot in shadows and then back to sunlight. If you can find a normally lit area of a play yard or even inside of a fairly nice-sized room, make use of that. Going back and forth is distracting and often times will change the color balance of the camera. Consistency is the key – you're selling the dog, and we need to keep the customer focus on the object we're selling. In Hollywood productions, thousands of dollars are spent to keep the consistency of a film, TV show or commercial. For us, an easy way to do this is to keep the scene as consistent as possible by limiting where we're shooting and the differences in light.

The idea is to be consistent in the overall video. If you move from light to dark, let it be done once and be consistent after that. If you go from inside to outside, let it be done once. Simple is better.

Make it a positive experience for everyone involved. This includes the dog and the person helping you. There is no need to overanalyze the production of the video or try to force the dog to do something that you think may be a *perfect scene*. Just shoot the footage and work with what you get. If you push too far, you will annoy the person helping you and/or the dog. I always have a lot of fun doing these videos and suggest you do the same.

*If I could go back in time
to when you were a little puppy,
a time before you knew the pain
that you now feel,*

*what could I tell you about your
future?*

I'm sorry...

Sharing is Caring

Sharing these videos is the key to their success, and it's really simple to do. I use email, Facebook, Twitter, YouTube and our Bound Angels newsletters. Also, the city shelters are now sending these videos out to their email networks, as well as placing a link to the videos on their websites. Certain shelter software such as Chameleon also allows the URL to be attached to the pet's information. The more eyeballs you can get onto your video, the better chance you have of *"selling your used dog."* That is why I say "keep it interesting."

I don't pay too much attention to how many views my video gets on YouTube – for a few reasons. I don't think all views get counted when a video is embedded on a certain page and, most importantly, because I don't care about views. I care about sales. I've seen dogs get adopted with 100 views and others not get anything after several hundred views. Get people to watch and see the trend for yourself – you'll start to see some patterns. I've found that even after a dog is adopted, people will still continue to watch the videos, and that is a good sign to me. I've seen some videos get hundreds of extra views once the dog already has a home. I think this shows that people are interested in what someone else got and that should inspire us to get busy on our next video.

I've also found that uploading a video to Facebook's video section in addition to YouTube is a good idea. For some reason, people are more likely to watch the video if it's local to the site they're on. Also, placing the video on several sites gets you more eyeballs on what you're selling.

If you can get your friends to send your masterpiece out to their friends, even better! The better your video, the more likely people are to share it with their friends. When asking friends to share your video, bear in mind that you cannot ask this favor every time. I use this as a tool when the dog is not getting adopted as quickly as I'd like.

Read my section on emailing in the next chapter, and notice I stress to send the original to yourself and then bcc everyone else. Your friends will appreciate you for this.

Social Networking vs. Email

With the advent of social networks such as YouTube, Facebook, Twitter and countless others that are all free, - there are more and more avenues available to help save animals and market them to an even wider audience. The benefit is that people will continue to talk and post about animals until the animal is adopted – sometimes beyond. Also, we can post follow-up stories about the adoption / adopter on a photo album, story, etc. Many people use email and send hundreds of emails a day about a particular dog. There are some upsides to this, but countless downsides.

I use the email option a last resort. First of all, I don't think people read their emails that much unless it's from someone they know and, secondly, there's a good chance your mail will end up in their spam folder. Some people begin to tune out after receiving many emails from the same person. There are certain people who have alienated me so much that I've created a spam filter solely for their emails. If you are going to use email, I would suggest a few things:

1. *Don't become an incessant nag*. There are countless people that I send straight to

my spam folder because they overdo emails. Some people will send so many emails that no one *ever* looks at them. That is a crime because the only ones that suffers here are the dogs they are trying to save. Even though these peoples' hearts are in the right place, they are not able to focus on a clear strategy – and *strategy sells dogs*. If you send out 100 emails a day, you're going to upset people and people will eventually tune you out. It's like the boy who cried wolf too many times.

2. ***Use a clear and concise subject line and make it interesting***. **DIES AT 4PM TODAY** is not a good subject line. It doesn't give the reader an option and makes the situation totally hopeless. I'm not saying the animal's life isn't important – I am saying that a last minute plea is overwhelming for most readers. To *sell used dogs* we have to focus on a positive aspect. ***Smiling Charlie Needs a Warm Heart*** makes a reader want to see what Smiling Charlie might look like. I use subject lines that spark people's interest. ***His ears are as big as his heart.***

3. ***Do NOT cc everyone, or anyone for that matter***. There is nothing people hate more than having their private email address shared with everyone in rescue. There is a **bcc** option and it should be used. If you

don't know how to **bcc**, ask someone to show you. And the excuse, *I forgot cause I was in a hurry*, just doesn't cut it. Respect your friends' privacy and they will respect your position. No matter how often I've mentioned this to certain people in rescue, they never listen. Eventually people start "replying to all" and hundreds of email addresses are on the list and the email becomes so confusing that no one knows where to begin. I've found myself scrolling through so much garbage to eventually get to the email that just hit delete. Emails should be clean, clear and concise.

4. *Keep track of the animal*. Whoever starts the email should continue to maintain a "point position" on the animal. Has the animal been adopted, killed or rescued? This "contact person" should be listed at the top of every email sent so that it is clear whom to contact. Have clear contact info in the body of the email. If you are forwarding the mail be certain that there is a contact email or phone number clearly visible in the mail. There is nothing more frustrating for the person trying to help than not being able to get in contact with the person responsible for the dog.

6. *Keep the email clean*. Focus on the facts and, if you're forwarding the email, be sure

to keep the focus of the email clear.

7. *Date the email in the body of the message*. When the animal is adopted, or rescued (or worse yet, killed), a message should be sent out to the group to update everyone. Oftentimes people continue to work on an animal after it has been saved or killed. This is valuable time that can be spent on the next pet. Everyone likes some good news, so be sure to share the good stories.

8. *SIZE MATTERS*. When people email a 4 meg picture, it takes forever to download and can't be seen on a normal computer, let alone a cell phone. If you're emailing pictures: *RESIZE is WISE*. The biggest the picture should measure is 900 pixels at its largest side. I make it a habit to name the pictures with the dog's name and animal ID#. For example: DollyA1234565-1. The second would be -2, and so on. Any image editing software will allow you to resize your pictures before you mail them.

Most of the animals that the *Bound Angels Shelter Angel Video Program* has saved have been as a result of social networking sites and personal contacts. Blind emails generally are not as powerful as we'd like to think. Plus sending an email out to 100,000 people is generally not going to help. Remember, the animal is local; there are shelters, rescue organization and animals needing help everywhere. I try to be as focused in my marketing as possible. I've sent dogs to other states and as far away as Canada, but there is a lot of work involved in doing that. It's advisable to keep your focus on a feasible area close enough to the shelter so that people can drive there to meet their new friend.

Those people who left you here
don't see your tears
and don't hear your cries,
but I do...

and that is why I am here.

The Shelter

How can we make the experience of the shelter better for the public? Let's face it – a shelter can be one of the most depressing places on earth for any animal lover. So, we have to focus on what can make it a little brighter. If money is no object (yeah right), we can make them beautiful, air-conditioned and have aromatherapy throughout. That, however, is not an option. So we need to focus on what we can do.

Here's a great way that rescue should help out shelters. Volunteers can spend a few hours a week cleaning the shelters, a fresh coat of paint; organize the front lobby and a host of other things can make the shelter more inviting.

During open hours the shelter should look its best so, if necessary, staff should clean the kennels before people walk through and be aware that they are not spraying the runs (or dogs) down as people walk by. Easy solution: before opening, clean and prepare – during opening hours SELL SELL SELL.

It is paramount that there ALWAYS is one person wandering the aisles of the shelter ready to help people who are looking for a pet. This can be a staff member or a volunteer who is able to show a prospective customer the pet they wish to see.

Another good idea is to have paper and pencils available at various posts so that people can write down the animal's info and bring it back to the staff. This can be as simple as golf-pencils and index cards.

Shelter staff should be focused on the goal at hand – **Selling Used Dogs**. This can be done through motivational and incentive-based programs as well. I'll discuss one that Bound Angels developed below. The primary focus of shelter managers must be placing *friendly sales people* on the *sales floor*. This means a courteous, helpful shelter staff. Shelter employees who relate best to the public should be outgoing and motivated to *sell used dogs*. Be sure that the people on the *sales floor* are motivated and positive.

One of the key elements to success is the ability to get help in order to adopt a pet. Walk through your local pet store and see how often an employee will ask, "Would you like to play with the puppy?" Now walk through your local shelter and try to find an employee to get a dog out.

Remember, this is sales. We're selling used dogs. How about if we equate it to a used car lot? How "helpful" is the salesperson? Imagine if we could only staff every shelter with one used-car salesman. Now, it's not that we need someone in a loud suit pushing the yellow lab, but it would be nice to be able to find a member of the staff or volunteer who will engage the customers.

Remember, the dogs are the merchandise, the adopters are the customers and the shelter staff or volunteers are the salespeople. Shelter managers should consider incentive-based programs. For two months, Bound Angels ran a promotion at one LA shelter in which we would give a $100 gift card to the employee with the most positive comment cards. The winner not only won $100, but she also adopted out more pets than anyone else **AND** the adoption numbers at that shelter shot up by nearly 30% for that month. This was a very successful program, and it was based on incentive.

If everyone is getting paid the same to do a little or a lot, most people will not spend too much more effort to work. Rewarding those who work hard makes more sense than punishing those who are doing very little. As anyone who knows anything about dog-training knows, reward-based training methods will get a dog to comply happily and build a better relationship with his or her person. And, since we can't use a prong collar on shiftless employees, focus on those that are doing the hard work and it might just jolt the others into doing the right thing, too.

If budget concerns are the issue, see if you can get a local restaurant, movie theater or store to donate a gift card. There are countless ways to reward employees who are doing a great job. Think outside the box!

Budget concerns are always the issue in shelters, yet managers often don't realize there are costs involved in housing pets at the shelter. Moving them out quickly saves money and it saves lives.

<u>*Give a Dog a Bone*</u>

One of the biggest problems we face in the shelter and trying to **Sell Used Dogs** is presentation. Dogs rushing to the front of a kennel and barking can scare off many "customers." How do we fix this? The solution is simple: **Give a Dog a Bone**. Several years back I would go to a particular shelter that housed many dogs that exhibited this behavior and I took the matter into my own hands. I would stop at a local warehouse store and buy a big box of dog biscuits. I would load up a canvas bag and walk through the shelter. As I approached a particular row of kennels I would watch for dogs that would run toward to front and start barking. Once they calmed down and sat or stood quietly only for a moment, I would drop a biscuit into the kennel.

This very simple principle in dog training and behavior is called reinforcement. I would "reward" the dog for "not barking – not lunging." The key thing here is *when* I give the dog the "bone." If the dog gets the bone when he is lunging and barking we are reinforcing that behavior – and we do **NOT** want to do that. This is a very good thing to train volunteers to do – dog walkers can do it as well. If the dog is acting nutty, don't continue. If you are about to open the kennel and the dog is acting crazy, wait. Once the dog is calm(er), then proceed. This may take a few minutes, but the key is not to give in. The crazier the dog acts, the longer we wait.

In a shelter environment this might be nearly impossible to do 100%, but any work is better than none. Do what you can and help the dogs become better citizens. Dogs that lunge at the front of their kennels have a very slim chance of adoption. People are afraid of them or feel threatened by them. The reason the dog is doing this is generally because the front of the kennel symbolizes two things: First, it is the way to freedom, and they want freedom. And second, it is a barrier that they may be guarding. If the dog barks and the person moves away, the barking is automatically reinforced.

There was a dog at a local shelter that would charge and bark every time someone would approach. He was a beautiful shepherd, and I was intrigued as to why he hadn't been adopted. I approached his kennel and he charged the gate and barked (quite fiercely I might add). He barked for a few minutes, although it seemed like a lot longer. I never moved. I never made eye contact. I stood still. Regressing was not an option. Once he became calm, I dropped a treat on the floor in front of him. He then came closer and looked at me, and I dropped another treat. I then touched the door and he barked again. I waited and when he stopped I dropped another treat. All of this took about 7 minutes or so. Eventually I opened the gate (much to the surprise of the kennel workers), he came forward, I slipped a leash over his head and we went out to the yard. He was a fabulous dog that I later placed in a youth dog-training program. He was a model citizen who completed the program and eventually got a great home – all because I didn't give up on him. I urge you to give these dogs a chance. Sometimes the greatest gems are hidden behind a clump of coal.

Dogs that exhibit behavior not in line with what we expect deserve a second chance, or at least a second look. Barking does not always indicate aggression. In fact many dogs will bite without ever sounding a bark. Barking can be alerting, playful, protective or fear-based. But retreating from a dog that is barking at a kennel door reinforces whatever weakness is in the dog's mind. There is a kennel door to protect us. If the dog lunges at the door with teeth bared, hackles up and an "I want to kill you attitude," you might not want to open the door, but barking and running toward the door is often nothing more than posturing. Waiting it out and reinforcing a behavior that we desire is a great way to help a dog along.

The concept of people *giving a dog a bone* through the bars of the kennel can play a key role in "re-socializing" a dog that has lost some of his manners. I do not advise children to do this, and I also do not advise people to place the treat into the dog's mouth. Dogs can become a bit "mouthy" ** when un-socialized and someone could get bit. The treat can simply be dropped onto the floor.

*** Mouthy is a term used to describe a dog that uses a bit too much force to get a treat from a person's hand. It doesn't mean aggressive in any way. Some dogs may be very submissive yet still take treats roughly. There are ways to teach a dog to be less mouthy, but since this is not a book on dog training, I won't go into them here. I would like to stress that just because a dog takes treats roughly, does not indicate that the dog is aggressive.*

I believe very strongly that a dog can be better acclimated to the shelter, and increase his chances of adoption, if he learns that people walking up to, or by his kennel, are not a danger or a threat. If every time a dog sees a person walk up to the front of his kennel, he barks and the person leaves, he is receiving reinforcement that what he is doing is okay. Train volunteers to spend some time each day dealing with this issue. This is one of the biggest problems facing shelter dogs and one of the easiest to fix. Some basic notes to doing this properly:

1. Do not show the dog the treat when approaching the kennel. We're not bribing him; we are rewarding him when he exhibits the right behavior. Also, if a dog sees the treat he may get very excited and that is counterproductive to what we are doing.

2. Do not talk to the dog. Remain still.

3. Do not regress or leave the front of the kennel while the dog is barking or acting nutty.

4. Do not stare into the dog's eyes. A slight gaze around the kennel is best.

5. When the dog calms down, drop the treat into the kennel immediately – do not delay. At this point you can say something soothing like, *"Yes"* or *"Good Boy."* Now wait and repeat the exercise. You can repeat this exercise by moving away and re-appearing.

6. By the time you leave, the dog should be relatively calm, looking toward you for another treat.

7. Do not do this exercise while other dogs or people are walking by, if at all possible.

8. Do not pet the dog. You are reinforcing his security with having people walk by his kennel, not touching him at this point.

9. Use treats that are big enough to be a reward, not morsels. It should take the dog a few seconds to eat the treat. Also, be careful the treat is not so big that it takes him too long to eat it or that one treat fills him up. For this reason, I don't use chicken jerky or chew treats. Regular dog biscuits work best and if you are working with a small dog, break them in half.

Ask Me About Fido

Since most shelters have color printers, there is a simple tool that can be used to get attention to particular animals. I call this *Ask me about Fido.* It's a fun program and can be put into place quite simply. Take a good picture of a dog and size it according to the dimensions of the pin-on badges that are sold at office supply stores. If the budget allows, buy a button maker and adjust the size accordingly.

A bright cheery picture of the dog worn by members of the staff will give the staff a more personal relationship with that animal, and it's a sales generator for customers walking into the shelter. Imagine every employee wearing a button with a dog's picture on it.

Yes, there are hundreds of dogs in the shelter and 10 employees wearing a button with a dog's picture on it may not get attention to all of the dogs, but it is a start. The buttons can be replaced or swapped around between employees on a regular basis, I prefer to have the same employee wear the same button until the dog gets adopted. They can even take them home and wear them when they are off from work. Then, as each dog is adopted, these buttons can be placed onto a bulletin board in the main lobby of the shelter. This is a great motivator and reward for those who *sold more used dogs* than anyone else. It is a reward for everyone, since each button on the board is a life saved.

Employees from all departments, as well as volunteers, should take part in this fun activity, and it should be a team effort. The more buttons on the board, the bigger the celebration. Keep the focus on the size of the board, not only on the person with the most buttons.

Accountability

The animal rescue world is an emotional
rollercoaster and many people get caught up
in it. This causes much strife between shelter
employees and the rescue community. If
these two don't work together, the system
will fall apart. There should be a symbiotic
bond between both in order to make the
system work. Hating the shelters because
they kill dogs makes no sense, nor does
hating rescuers because they're emotional
and can be a pain in the butt. The shelter can
only kill the dogs that people drop off to
them, so hate the people who bring their
dogs to the shelter.

We need to keep the focus on the problem
and solving it, as that is the goal of this
book. We can go on a tangent and blame the
system, irresponsible breeders and the
government for the overcrowded shelters
that are killing millions of pets, but that will
not solve anything. Each person makes a
conscious decision to keep a pet for its life
or not – the blame rests solely with that
person. Occasionally there are exceptions,
such as a dog that belonged to someone who
has fallen ill or died and there is no one to
care for that pet – this is the rarest of
exceptions. If we could solve the other
issues, these pets would have a safe refuge

in our shelters for as long as it would take to find them a forever home. Accountability is what I like to refer to as self-responsibility. Often, I hear of people going into shelters with the best of intentions. They want to save all the animals – every animal they see is another tragedy. These people overextend themselves and become so overwhelmed that they end up less productive than if they focused on one task at a time.

I remember dealing with an adoption coordinator at one of the local shelters. It got to be a hectic two weeks. It was never my goal or the goal of Bound Angels to do "hands on adoptions." We're not set up with fosters, adoption events or any other program that could help in the actual placing of animals. During this two-week period an abundance of animals needed my help. I put my name on these animals and it ended up being more than I thought possible to help. I had no place to put them and no hope in sight. Thank God for the Shelter Angel Videos (see the chapter on these videos). I gave my word to Larry that I would save all five; all I asked is that he give me until a particular day. He was reluctant to do so, as he knew it was a monumental task. On the last day, I pulled out the last dog – *Large Marge #1* and Larry shook my hand and acknowledged how rare it was that someone follows through like this. Large Marge was a dog that Larry was particularly attached to (who says shelter workers don't get attached to dogs?) and she is now a therapy dog working with handicapped children.

The key thing I try to remember is what I was told by a rescuer when I first started: "Every time you ask the shelter to spare the life of the animal that you are trying to save, you're asking them to kill another one." I take that very seriously. My goal is to eliminate that option at all costs. If you are accountable to the shelter you are working with, the shelter will be willing to work with you. If your dealings with the shelters are easy, the shelter will deal better with you. The same thing holds true for the shelter staff. As a shelter employee, it's your job to deal with animals and people – and particularly people who are trying to save animals. Lay your rules down and make them clear. If you are giving a person three days to take a particular animal, there should be notes in the system as well as on the animal's cage that the animal is on HOLD. There should be no errors. Every option should be given to a pet that has the possibility to be saved. These dogs are not more special than those with no one, but they do have a chance.

You look away from me because
on the surface I look like the
human that left you here.

But look a little deeper, for I am
not that person...

I am here to save you.

Good Use of the PA System

Studies show that listening to soft, classical music can affect dogs in a positive way, by calming them down. If your kennel has a PA system that is not used unless someone is being paged, rethink its value. And, if you don't have a PA system, see if you can get an old stereo donated, or even some boom-boxes placed on chairs in the kennels.

The best music I have found is natural sounds (eliminating thunderstorms of course), calming spa type music or classical-easy listening music without vocals. I've used this approach in training dogs that may get into drive by seeing other dogs walking by a window, gate or other areas.

The first objection many people have is that the shelter is so noisy that you can't hear the music over the barking of the dogs. This is no reason to blast the music or eliminate this concept, because it's the chicken/ egg theory. There is always a time when all dogs in a kennel are quiet – I can attest to this. There is also that time when they immediately get into drive. The use of soft, calming music is there to bridge the gaps and return the dogs to a calmer state more quickly. If calm music is playing, it will lower the dogs' reactivity to triggers and stress – therefore making them more prone to return to a calm state much quicker.

The music should be played at a comfortable level, not so loud as to drown out the barking. Dogs will pick up on this and become acclimated to the sounds. It may take time, but using this tool is a powerful way to give dogs a resource to focus on that will reduce their stress. The same play-list can be used over and over again; I don't think dogs get tired of songs. There are so many selections of easy listening music, soundscape CDs and downloads. There are also Internet radio stations that can be piped into the kennels that focus on particular genres.

Placement of Pets

With the attitude of many rescue organizations, I would be very unlikely to be approved to adopt a dog from them. Why do I say that? Because most rescue groups make it so unrealistic to adopt a dog that they end up stockpiling them while millions die at the shelters. If you are reading this and feel offended, look at your adoption policies and home-check criteria. The goal of rescue is to place pets and keep them from being killed in shelters. If you are spending weeks or months lining up home checks and screening through potential applicants who have the ultimate perfect home, you may be one of the people at the root of the problem.

Yes, every pet should go to a perfect home, but what is a perfect home? A big house with a nice yard, a large fence, manicured lawn, no gate the dog could escape through, two people living together with no other pets that may bother the new dog, not near any busy streets, no stairs that might be hard on the dog's legs when he gets old, and the list goes on and on. **Let's face it: these animals are living on cement floors with no beds and steel bars for windows. Life isn't going get that much worse.** And for those people who say, "There are some things worse than death…" I invite you to check in with the dog first.

To be realistic in placing pets, we need to lighten up on our hopes of the "perfect home" for every pet and focus instead on a "good home" for all pets. Many people may not know exactly what we expect of them and would be open to learning more about what they need to do in order to provide a better home for a potential pet.

There should be a series of questions to ask potential adopters to see if the dog would fit into their lifestyle. For example, a high-energy dog that requires much exercise would not be a good fit in a home with retired people or handicapped people. A dog that is high strung is not a good match for a home with small children, as it may easily run them over. Mellow dogs and dogs with respiratory issues should not be adopted by someone who is looking for a running partner. Be smart on the questions you pose.

A story comes to mind that breaks my heart. Gilly was a dog at a local shelter. I was referred an adopter through a local rescue. They said they had the perfect home for him. They had done a home-check, the lady had previously had a similar dog and he (Gilly) reminded her so much of that dog that she just could not wait to get him. I met

Gilly at the shelter and noticed immediately that he was very shy and timid. I asked if the lady was okay with that. I was told that the woman had experience in dealing with these issues and was a very responsible dog owner; I need not worry. I asked her to follow some basic instructions on introducing Gilly to her cat, new people etc. The person who vouched for this adopter assured me of everything. Well a few months later I got a phone call which froze me in my tracks. The woman (experienced dog owner that she was) had several issues with Gilly chasing cats and killing two of them, including her own. She never consulted a trainer nor did any work to curb this behavior – especially after the first dead cat. What she did do was take Gilly to her vet and kill him. This story is horribly disturbing and I'm only stating it here to show that even the best homes can turn out badly. I've seen countless dogs placed into homes that other rescuers would not approve of, and these dogs are living happy healthy lives. Basically, it's all a crapshoot. You have to take the good with the bad and understand that, as a numbers game, animals will 100% certainly be killed in shelters; their chances are inevitably better in a home.

Our goal as rescuers is to give these animals a chance. If we block that chance, we are most certainly condemning them to death. And, as I stated above – for those who wish to play God and say, "There are fates worse than death" – I urge them to think of which fates come to mind. For the most part, there are none that come to my mind: death is inescapable. Bad situations can be remedied – death cannot!

As rescue workers, we understand that we do our best. Sometimes we fail – sometimes we succeed. We must stay focused on the task at hand and keep our eye on the ball. The more time we spend focused on the individual battles, the less time we can spend trying to win the war. Do not let your setbacks get you down. Take them in stride and understand that you are doing work that you probably had no hand in creating. Every animal that is killed in a shelter is the fault of the person who gave up on them, whether that is because they couldn't care for them, got tired of them, or never gave enough effort to be sure that the animal would fit into their lives. The fault rests solely on these individuals. I only wish that these people could be forced to see the lifeless bodies that are carried out the back door of our shelters every day.

They come in on a leash and leave in a barrel.

We are the warriors – the true warriors who fight for the voiceless – our war is a war of compassion and caring. Stand up tall and understand that you truly are fighting a battle that is more worthwhile than any war we've fought, because we are fighting for innocent lives that cannot speak for themselves.

Our voice is their voice.

I've never met you before today,
but I'm here to help you.

I don't know why – but I know I must.

Driving People into Shelters
Driving Pets out of Shelters

One of the primary goals that I had in creating Bound Angels was to get people into the shelters: this differs from rescue groups who focus on getting pets out of shelters. My goal was twofold and relates primarily to the general public. Bound Angels would create awareness to the plight of the pets in the shelter. The more we could spread this message, the more pets we could get out of shelters. Yes, we can get dogs to mobile adoptions and adoption events, but we are limiting the merchandise to what we bring with us. Plus, the awareness of the shelter situation is one of the keys to solving this crisis.

If a shelter takes 20 dogs to an adoption there are still 200 at the shelter. And since each one is different, we never know what the customer is going to want. Walking through the shelter is similar to going shopping at a huge department store. Each dog is different, which is such a great sales tool. At a pet store the dogs are limited to specific breeds and will look just like the other dogs of that breed. Shelter dogs are unique – and unique sells.

One thing that shelter workers need to focus on when dealing with customers is the unique factor of their merchandise. The breeders and the pet stores have the exact same merchandise – each animal looks the same. *"If you want to be just like everyone else, visit the breeder, but if you are as unique as our pets – you've come to the right place."*

Of course the statement in the paragraph above is only partially true. We all know that about 20% of our stock consists of purebred dogs. The issue is that these dogs aren't that difficult to move out of the shelter. We need to focus on the ones that no one is looking at and create awareness and interest in them. We can use the purebred dogs as our "loss-leaders," but we want to bring attention to the wonderful mixed breed dogs that make up most of our stock. ***Loss-leaders*** are what department stores advertise to get customers into their stores so that they can sell the merchandise where they will make a profit. Loss-leaders are just that, something to get people in. The store is losing money on each one of these items they sell – obviously they need to sell something else.

This is why I find it paramount that rescue organizations work with shelters and rescue animals at risk of death, not those at risk of adoption. When rescue organizations run to shelters to snatch up the young purebred puppy and leave the middle-aged and older dogs, they are not helping the situation all that much. In fact, I feel that they hurt it. The young dogs, cute dogs and pure-bred dogs will most certainly get adopted if the shelter follows the protocols of marketing and outreach. There are countless dogs that are on the death list because they have issues or are overlooked, and it is these dogs that need rescue to step up for them.

If we are going to *rescue*, we need to focus on the animals that are at risk of death. If an animal is recently up for adoption, we should see if the shelter can adopt it out through its channels and focus instead on those animals that are on the short list.

I remain strong,
I wipe away my tears when I work.

But at the end of the day my tears
flow,
some for those I could not save
and some tears of joy for the lives
I have saved…

Sale-ability

The cars are all gleaming in the parking lot, the flags are blowing and it's time to make a deal. How does _your_ merchandise stack up? If you want someone to _want_ something (a used dog in this case) you have to make it "want-able."

- _Is the dog clean?_
- _Does he have a bandana on?_
- _Is there a place on the kennel for a sheet of paper with his picture and a small story about him?_
- _Does he have a clever name?_
- _Is there someone available to take him out to introduce him to his potential new family?_

The bottom line is _we need to focus on sales_ if we want to save lives. The best thing we can do is to understand that if _we're not selling – animals are dying._ There's a great line from Glengarry Glen Ross, "_Remember ABC – Always Be Closing._" Well our motto has to be, "Always Be Selling." **_Sales Save Lives_**. If we are not on the sales floor, which in our case is walking the aisles of the kennels, animals will be killed to make room. If even one person is in the shelter, we should greet them and if they "just want to look around," they should know we are available when they need us.

When greeting someone it's good to say, "If you'd like to see one of our furry friends, just let me know, I'd be happy to bring any one out for you to play with." There is no job in the shelter more important than helping a prospective adopter. Don't kid yourself into thinking that cleaning, feeding, paperwork or anything match up. None of these things will save a life like sales.

Sales Save Lives

Matching Volunteers with Dogs

One of the best ways to keep dogs and people safe is to make certain that the right dogs are matched to the right volunteers for walking, playing and showing them to the public. If a person is older, smaller or weaker, it is probably a good idea not to have them handle a 100-lb dog that is bound to pull them over. To avoid this, we use a system of dog and volunteer rating. The color ranking system is the easiest way to enforce this.

Green: Any small dog, no issues, medium and large dogs that don't pull or lunge toward people or other dogs. Dogs that are non-confrontational even when challenged.

Yellow: Dogs with minor issues. These may be easily distracted, but don't become reactive. They pull slightly on the leash, but re-direct easily. They listen to the handler and respond well to treats or slight corrections.

Red: Dogs that are highly reactive to other dogs, people or their environment. Red dogs are not always aggressive dogs, but dogs with aggression issues can be categorized into this rank. Dogs that have a high level of play drive and cannot easily be controlled, dogs that don't focus well as well as very large stubborn dogs.

Simply stated, volunteers are ranked with the same color system.

Red Volunteers are very dog-savvy people that can handle any situation. They are strong enough to control dogs that might be reactive and have the ability and knowledge to work with more than one dog. Red Volunteers are allowed to handle any of the three ranked dogs.

Yellow Volunteers are those that have some experience with dogs and are involved in learning more. They can handle a dog and give a fair correction to a dog. These volunteers are also able to "read" a dog to see if there might be a problem. They have the ability and the sense not to introduce dogs that they don't think will get along. Yellow volunteers are permitted to handle all GREEN and YELLOW dogs.

Green Volunteers are the newcomers and are still in training or are weaker, younger or older. They cannot handle a dog that pulls or may need some slight corrections. They are allowed only to play with the dogs and walk the dogs that are rated Green.

Some people may get their egos involved and become upset at being rated a rank below what they feel they deserve. This is put into place in order to protect both dogs and people. I have heard nightmare stories of well-intentioned volunteers accidentally letting two large dogs get together and the introduction ended in the death of both dogs. *Red Volunteers* have a big responsibility and this should not be taken lightly. They can also be used to mentor and train new volunteers and work with those at the green level. Re-evaluations can be done on a regular basis in order to get more volunteers into higher positions.

It is imperative for the safety of everyone that shelters focus on evaluating dogs and volunteers to work with the dogs that may have issues and not allow the issues to get worse.

Every shelter should have at least one person on-staff during public hours whose sole responsibility it is to walk the kennel aisles looking for potential customers. If the staff is too slim, get a volunteer to do it or, at the very least, put a sign in the kennel aisles that says, *"If you'd like to meet one of our loving pets, please come to the front counter and we will be happy to introduce you."* Make it friendly and make it easy.

For some reason shelters are seen as the neighborhood dogcatcher, and that is a stereotype we need to lose. Shelters should be seen as the first place people go to adopt a new friend. The only way we will do this is to make them friendlier, and we make them friendlier by providing better customer service.

Starting today, shelters should put down the hat of the dogcatcher and put on the face of **America's Pet Superstore**. There are no pet stores, not even the largest ones, which have the amount, or the variety of, pets that the local shelter has. Our prices are lower, our merchandise is more diverse. It's almost like we have a monopoly – but we are not being smart. We have never looked at ourselves as salespeople – we need to change that. We need to have banners, advertise, market, and we need to make sure that when customers come to our "store" that we are there to help. The more we focus on **Selling Used Dogs**, the easier we will find a solution to our dilemma. *Focusing on the solution is the answer.*

The Binary Dog

If you are reading this on your computer, you are aware of the unlimited power that your computer holds. It can compute complicated numerical equations, edit 3-D movies, compose a symphony, play complex video games, and write simple letters. In fact, some of you may be reading this on a phone or tablet that can do the same. All of these things are accomplished with a simple basic starting point, *1's and 0's*. All of the most complicated things that your computer does are broken down into 1's and 0's and through this basic fundamental system, all of the complex things your computer does can be accomplished. This is called the *binary code*.

Training a dog and understanding how a dog thinks can be broken down just as simply.

Your dog lives in the black and white. If we wish to understand our dogs better and communicate better with them, we need to walk in the middle. Many people think this *middle* is the grey, but it's not – it is the line *between* the black and white. It is the point upon which we stand that allows us to jump from black *to* white without hesitation. In fact, it is neither black nor white, but the place of choice.

To break this concept down into rudimentary terms, let's start our inter-species communication with the binary code of *YES* and *NO*. If the dog does something we like or approve of, we say YES and give the dog a treat to reinforce that the *YES* is a positive. Since dogs do not speak English, we will teach them through the use of a reward (i.e., treat)" that YES is good. By the same token, we need to teach the dog that NO is disapproval, and in order to do that we will withhold the reward (sort of a punishment).

Simple:

YES is good. GOOD = Reward
NO is "not" good. NOT GOOD = No
Reward

A simple way to put this method into play is to watch a dog that is exhibiting negative behavior – for example jumping or barking. As long as the dog jumps and barks, we do not reward the dog. Contrary to this is the belief that yelling NO will make him stop. Yelling at a dog is a reinforcement that may put the dog further into *drive*. Instead of adding to the negative behavior, we can ignore the dog's action by not giving him reinforcement, such as yelling or hitting. Even a negative reinforcement such as yelling, hitting, or squirting a dog with water can, and does, serve as a type of reinforcement in his mind – be it negative or positive.

If a dog is exhibiting a powerful drive such as aggression, this method will probably not work, but this binary communication technique will develop the building blocks of communication instead of solutions to complex behaviors. I would add that by using building blocks now, complex behaviors will be much easier to solve later on.

When a dog is jumping, we simply wait for the dog to stop the behavior and say YES. Then give the dog a treat. The dog instantly starts to relate that the word YES and the treat mean the same thing – APPROVAL. When starting out with dogs that are not exhibiting negative behaviors, we can simply give the dog a treat and a YES for looking at us, sitting or being calm. After all, calm behavior is something we want to reward. Most people enforce the negative with NO's and

OFF. If we focus on rewarding positive behaviors, dogs will be more likely to offer them.

The *binary* approach is the simplest method for the dog to understand, and the easiest for us to apply. Instead of trying to get the dog to understand that you are upset because of his actions and trying to make him do what you want him to do, it becomes a matter of – 1's and 0's – **YES** or **NO.** You either like what the dog is doing or you don't.

If you like what your dog is doing, he gets a treat and a YES,
If you don't like it, he gets nothing and a short NO.

It's important to note that the NO is not a firm, yelling or angry NO. It's more of a *NOPE*. If you put too much emphasis on the NO, it starts to carry more weight than the YES. Remember, it's the way we say things that the dog understands – more so that what we are actually saying. If we yell the NO, *that* is reinforcement in and of itself. The YES must carry more of a meaning and can be a happy-jolly-excited YES. Many times women will have an easier time adding emotion and men will have an easier time expressing disappointment. It is important for us to balance our emotions when it comes to dog training. This means expressing ourselves in a way the dog can understand.

Dogs live in the present and if we truly understand *that,* we can appreciate that we must reward or punish in the NOW. If a dog did something negative or positive even five seconds ago, the NOW is gone. If a dog is jumping and stops for a second –reward that action NOW with an enthusiastic YES and a treat. Also, if a dog makes a movement toward a negative behavior and doesn't follow through – for example he goes for your favorite shoe and you say NO and he stops, reward *that* immediately. If you don't praise his accomplishments as soon as they happen, you're not rewarding the positive steps. Your dog can get confused if you don't include the YES *and* the NO. Using only YES' gives a dog a one-sided perspective as to what you want or expect.

People often think that dogs can be trained in either a solely positive or purely corrective training method – this could not be further from the truth. Although I don't agree with over-correcting dogs, I do believe that a firm correction, properly placed, is not only fair but also necessary when dealing with certain negative behaviors. Remember, dogs live in the black and white. They understand that there is a payment or punishment for each and every one of their actions.

When setting out to train a dog or changing his behavior, we need to start with the basics of the *binary system*. We need to lead the dog along the path of what he is doing and find his stumbling blocks. As we approach each stumbling block, we need to teach the dog positive and negative. If he's heading in a direction that we like, we approve and reward – if he's heading in a direction that we don't like, we disapprove and punish. (In most cases the punishment need not be more severe than the withholding of praise or reward.). This method can be used to lure and shape behaviors by rewarding *little steps* along the way to complex exercises. At each step, we reward the dog for the movement or action that is positive, and later we can chain these actions together by withholding the intermittent rewards for an ultimate reward at the end of the completed task.

Using this simple approach to training your dog will give you an advantage in understanding how to shape behaviors into those that you like. It can be a fun game to play with your dog on a daily basis. I use this approach in almost every situation I'm called upon to fix.

- When it's time for a walk, the leash doesn't get attached to the collar until the dog is calm and sitting down.
- If my dog tries to run out the door ahead of me, I close the door.
- I don't put my dog's food down until he sits and waits.
- My dog doesn't get petted until he sits calmly in front of me.
- I don't open the door to my dog's crate if he's crying or carrying on.

All of these exercises are part of the *binary code* of YES and NO. No matter how complex something may seem, remember it's made up of two simple things – YES and NO. Focus on the positive aspect and reward it. Shape the negative toward the positive and start to reward *that*. Eventually you will begin to see all behaviors as 1's and 0's - YES' and NO's.

I believe that all training should be fair to the dog. Since the dog has an unfair disadvantage in that we are trying to teach him *our* system, we must strive to make learning easy and fun for him. Giving a dog only two directions to move toward makes the path much clearer than a complex expectation. Remember, your dog doesn't know what you want if you don't teach him. Don't expect your dog to be a mind reader. Whether you are approaching the training of your first dog or you have had dogs your entire life, try using the *binary system* and see how fair training can be for both you and your dog.

B.A.R.C.
Behavioral Assessment & Reactivity Checklist

Developed by: Robert Cabral -
Bound Angels / Black Belt Dog Training

The premise of the canine temperament test has been widely disputed among animal rights people due to the unfair elements imposed on the dog. The primary reason for this controversy is the blanket "pass or fail" method that is applied to the outcome of the test. Assessing a dog's behavior should not be gauged *pass or fail*; rather we should strive to define the dog's behavior. We must use the test as a litmus to understand the dog's true temperament. To more clearly understand this, let's define the term "temperament."

To equate the word to a human level, we can define temperament as a dog's "personality." Seeing it in these terms, we should be able to clearly define what a dog's strong and weak traits are, and how to properly address them. For example, a dog that is fearful of other dogs or even dominant toward them is not a dog that should be put down, but it would be good to know this information before placing him into a home with other dogs, or with a weak handler. Rather, this dog should be placed with a rescue organization that could work at rehabilitating the dog. If we can assess a dog's needs, we can offer better solutions to place him in an environment best suited for him.

Although this test is designed to be as detailed as possible, we must understand that a dog is a living, breathing, ever-changing animal that may react one way during a test and differently once placed in a different environment. A great example of this is the likelihood of a dog acting more dominant around a weaker handler and less dominant around someone who is firmer. Dogs are conditioned by their environment, as well as by the people and animals that surround them.

If a test were performed in a completely sterile environment, the results would be useless because we never place our dogs in a truly sterile environment. The test is designed to give us a snapshot of a dog's personality, and as responsible people we must use this information in the best interest of the dog being tested.

It is my contention that few, if any dogs,

should ever be killed because of aggression issues. More than 90% of dominance and aggression can be treated through proper behavior modification by a qualified trainer or behaviorist. Much of this can be done with positive, reward-based methods, but we should not rule out correction-based training if it is the sole option to saving a dog's life. I would rather put a correction upon a dog than a needle in his vein. To say otherwise is playing God for an animal that deserves every option before a last resort.

My contention is that all training should start with a treat and a toy; where it goes from there is up to the individual dog. Training a dog, that is, teaching dog basic commands (i.e., sit, stay, down, come, etc.) should only be done through motivational methods. Enforcement of commands once we know the dog understands what we want can employ well-suited corrections, as long as they are fair to the dog. My opinion is that a correction is merely a *direction* for a dog to do what I'm trying to get him to do. For example, if a dog that I'm handling is pulling toward another dog and I say, NO, I can give a leash correction to take the dog away from that situation, thereby "correcting" him into compliance.

Thousands of dogs are killed every year for a plethora of reasons, some of which include bad behavior. If even a small percentage of them could be saved by proper behavioral evaluations, our work will be worthwhile. Furthermore, if we can offer another small percentage of these dogs another chance at life by instilling good behavior into them, it would be the greatest gift. All too often, people approach dogs with a blanket opinion, such as, "If the dog will not change his behavior through positive based methods, he will not change." Others say that correction-based training doesn't retain its strength. I would argue that, with much experience to the contrary. I have trained many dogs with correction-based methods (because the motivational techniques would not work due to the immense drive of the particular dog) and these dogs have maintained their good behavior over many years. These dogs showed serious aggression issues prior to training and are now living happy lives.

We must step outside of our egos and give the dog what he needs, not what we think he needs.

A word of caution to those performing the behavioral assessment test: Working with a dog that exhibits dominant or aggressive behaviors cannot be compared to performing a test on an unknown dog. Dogs can behave erratically or out of control during a behavioral assessment. There is an inherent risk of being bitten during a test, so extreme caution should be used. Do not let your guard down during any part of the test.

A note on underlying issues: There are several things that can sway a dog negatively in a behavioral assessment test, and it's imperative that they be addressed here:

A dog should not be tested immediately upon entering the shelter. The dog is in a highly stressed state and may react out of confusion. A test conducted on a dog within 12-24 hours of entering the shelter is not deemed valid. Dogs that are sick, including kennel cough or after any surgery requiring anesthesia, should not be tested until they are well or at least 48 hours after surgery. If recovery is necessary (for example, setting a broken bone or major surgery) the dog must be fully recovered, with no touch sensitivity before testing. If the dog is tested with stitches or staples still intact, the area in question must be avoided.

Dogs should not be tested immediately after feeding time and should not be removed from feeding for testing. Furthermore, a dog should not be tested in the proximity of other dogs that are eating.

Dogs should not be tested in the immediate vicinity of kennel mates still in the kennel. If dogs have issues with hip dysplasia, this issue should be taken into account and disclosed on the test.

The Tester: Having performed hundreds of these tests, I can confirm that no dog will respond the exact same way to two different people. In order to be fair to the dog, we must be sure that the dog has no blanket issue with the person performing the behavioral test. When I say blanket issue, I mean overly negative or positive. The best person to conduct a test is a person who can detach himself or herself from the task at hand and handle a dog neutrally.

If a dog really seems to like someone, that person may be likely to get inaccurate results on some parts of the test;

however, a negative pre-association to the tester is the most important aspect we should focus to avoid.

The tester's background need not to be a medical one. Some trainers make great testers - some don't. Some people may be too wishy-washy to deal with a strong dog at a moment's notice, while others are so dominant in tone that they cannot get a dog to relax enough in order to be playful or to exhibit his true personality. The tester must be neutral to "his favorite breed." Playing favorites or skewing a test because the handler is not a fan of the breed is unfair and has no place in a behavioral test. The level of energy spent dealing with the first dog should be the same as with the last; therefore it is advisable to consider how many tests the person can perform before requiring a break or ending testing for a given day. I've tested 15-20 dogs in a 3-4 hour time frame, for a basic test, while other dogs have consumed many hours over several days in order to get a fair idea of the dog's personality.

The tester is equally capable as a man or a woman and most any age. I look for a couple of qualifications for the person doing the test. The most important is the person's ability to read a dog. This generally comes with much experience in dealing with dogs that may have personality disorders. Dog trainers who spend most of their time in clients' homes often don't have the ability to read a dog that may exhibit behavioral issues – be they good or bad.

The attire of the person testing should allow them to interact freely with the dog. I generally wear jeans, boots and a t-shirt. If a person has sensitive skin, I suggest wearing a long-sleeved shirt or thin jacket to avoid getting scratched. Bulky clothes will inhibit movement, and freedom of movement is imperative when interacting with the dog. The reason I suggest a firm shoe or boot is that some dogs may become nippy at feet, and sneakers or sandals will leave our feet open to the dogs' "attacks" - regardless of if they are playful or serious. I also suggest avoiding clothing that makes rustling noises (such as nylon jackets) as this may distract a dog during the test.

The tester should be strong enough to control a dog at a moment's notice and compassionate enough to give each dog tested a fair chance.

The Testing Environment: Testing a dog at a shelter is not a perfect scenario. There are so many smells and sounds that trigger a dog to react in a way that may sway the test. This sway can be for the good or bad. Some dogs may respond aggressively in this environment and passively in a more neutral environment. Therefore, when testing at a shelter, I advocate for a field or area away from the medical, exam and intake area – as well as away from the main kennel area of the shelter whenever possible. If this is not possible, try to be as far away as you can..

How the dog is brought to the testing area will also influence the outcome. I suggest that a dog be brought from its kennel to the test area in a neutral manner. There should be no talking, petting or jerking the dog around. If the dog decides to engage in cage fighting, move the dog straight along. Correcting the dog incites a behavior in his mind that will sway the test, as well as his experience with the handler.

My initial method to meeting the dog to be tested is to approach the kennel, give the dog a treat or just drop a treat on the floor of the kennel and stand there for a brief moment. I always use a noose to secure the dog, generally luring him to the front of the kennel and then taking him out. If he is skittish, I will enter the kennel and noose him from there – again, my attitude remains very aloof. No matter how fearful or dominant the dog acts, I do not engage in any dialog or training methods at this point. If the dog is posturing, I do not approach him straight on; instead I approach from the side.

I do not like to use a catchpole on a dog, and up to now have never felt the need to use one in a test. The experience of the pole places a negative imprint on the dog that will impact the results of our test. If the dog cannot be safely handled by use of a simple noose, we need to give the dog more time or bring him into an area where he can be handled with a noose.

Once the dog is on the rope, we walk past the other dogs and get to the training or testing area as quickly as possible, and with as little drama as possible.

Once in the testing area, I leave the leash on the dog and allow him to run free for a few moments. If you are using a simple noose leash, I suggest you tie a knot above the ring to avoid the dog slipping out or getting his feet tangled. Some of the shepherd's leashes have a small piece of leather that can be slipped down to avoid loosening of the collar. In either case, I prefer to leave the dog on the leash during the entire test; I suggest you do the same.

More than likely, the dog will enjoy this initial bit of freedom and we can see if he runs up to other people in the testing area (although they should remain neutral and not engage the dog). He may also become fixated on something or he may need to relieve himself.

Possession test: At this point I want to see how possessive the dog is over a particular toy or object. Is his possessiveness over a particular toy or is he possessive over anything that he believes is his? The key to testing possessiveness with a dog is to always offer him another toy or reward of equal or greater value when trying to remove the first object. Just trying to yank a toy from a dog's mouth does not prove possessiveness, at least not on the dog's side. Offering him other items shows his dedication to the object he is currently dealing with. Also, if this item has him fixated, I may re-introduce it later to see if he will *lock* onto it again.

Most dogs are able to strike an object with a bite if it is moving in a normal *charged* manner. A big mistake people make is moving an item in an erratic manner when introducing it to the dog. The dog may inadvertently bite the skin or hand of the handler and thereby fail his test. This is not a failure for the dog, but more a failure of the handler. Introducing an item on a string that we can toss or *activate* on the ground serves as the best introduction of a toy. Furthermore, if I activate the toy, that is pull on it while the dog has a hold on it, the dog's natural instinct will be to pull back. You will not get an object out of a dog's mouth by pulling on it against the dog's grip, nor will you free the object by having someone yanking back on the dog while you are holding the object. The way to free the object through compulsion is to use a collar correction from the front of the dog while pulling or holding onto the object. However, I do not do this during a temperament test, as this leads into training and behavior modification. The idea of a test is to remain neutral.

Dogs that go from toy to toy are perfectly suited in normal behavior and show a high level of curiosity. Dogs that fixate on an object and cannot be pulled away from that object – no matter what the secondary reward is – are quite rare but show a strong dedication and drive. Dogs that bite or attack when approached while playing need to be schooled in the proper etiquette of play. This is not a reason to kill a dog; it's merely a personality trait that generally can be fixed.

There are different approaches to separating a dog from the object he is possessing:

- Remove the object from the dog while securing (or having another person secure) the dog. Offer a second item to the dog to make a swap.

- The best method is not to remove the item from the dog, but instead remove the dog from the item. If I use this method, I can bring the dog back to the item and see if his level of drive or possessiveness has gone up, down or remained the same.

If a dog growls when approached while playing with an item, he is exhibiting resource-guarding tendencies. These tendencies are prevalent in strong personality dogs and can often be quite useful in bite sports. If a dog snaps when approached, a correction should be delivered and the situation should be repeated.

Dogs that resource-guard to an extreme extent can be retrained through both motivational- and correction-based training. Although it is a rare trait in all but a few dogs, resource-guarding is a behavioral issue that needs to be addressed. What is important here is to clearly differentiate between a dog that is truly guarding to attack, from one that is growling in a manner to initiate continuation of play. This can generally be observed by noting the body language of the dog: Still body, hackles up, stiffness and eyes peering up are signs the dog is guarding and remaining possessive over the item. Loose energy, flexible body and mid-level growling while moving away from the item or holding it is a general indication that he wishes the game to continue.

Next, I will introduce a few toys, tugs or treats to see how the dog responds. I watch how the dog responds to me, the environment and to each item that I bring out of my bag as I retain an indifferent attitude. I do not start a play session with the dog at this point. I am merely looking at the dog's curiosity or drive toward the items I am handling. Is he excited, curious, pushy or indifferent?

I will throw a toy and see if he chases it, then I will throw another toy. Does he immediately go for the other toy and forget about the first? If not, I will approach him and offer him a treat or another toy from my hand to see if he'll give up the current toy. If not, I will grab hold of the toy and hold it. I do not pull it, jerk it or tug on it. I merely deaden the object. The best toy to use for this is a tug or ball on a string.

To avoid getting bitten, I secure a hold of the leash or noose the dog has been wearing the entire time. When you deaden an object, a dog will generally lose interest and let go. If he lets go, I throw it for him again and let him chase it. This shows that a dog has a natural prey drive and he is acting very normal. A dog that holds onto a toy that I have secured in my hand is not necessarily an aggressive dog; instead he is showing an engagement to me.

If a dog snaps when you grab the toy he is holding, this could be seen as aggression or "re-biting" – something a dog does to get a firmer hold on the object. If the dog "re-bites" the object, keep the object motionless and see he loses interest. A dog may "re-bite" an object a number of times before losing interest. If the dog snarls, growls or postures when you handle the object, we see this as a dominant tendency and he should be given a fair correction to see if he responds. Failing a dog due to possessiveness without offering him a fair correction is throwing the baby out with the bathwater. It is our job to read a dog for his personality, and some dogs require a slight correction to fall into line. If the dog becomes aggressive or continues his dominance, he is showing some tendencies toward possessiveness.

Depending on the level of the dog's possessiveness, I will present another object to the dog to see if he feigns interest in it. When testing a dog for possessiveness, we should see what the dog is possessive toward (food, toys, etc.). A dog with possession issues will continue to be possessive over an object even if we think he's lost interest in it. In his mind, he sees everything as his and no one can touch any of his possessions. That is why using multiple objects as a replacement gives us insight as to the dog's true drive.

Although there are ways to separate the item from the dog in a compulsive manner, we should not be concerned with this during a temperament test. If we can't get the item away from the dog during the test with the above explanation(s), then one of two things is true:

1. We are not qualified to handle this particular dog.

2. The dog is truly a difficult dog and should be rescue only and placed in a behavior modification program.

I would venture to say that more than likely #1 holds true for most situations. Unless a dog assaults with a bite or attack for trying to get the object away from him, there are many ways to get the object away from him. Please see previous sections of this book for more detailed explanations.

The touch / handling test: To start, we should understand that dogs don't generally like to be handled –that is often the reason why children get bit by dogs when they crawl on top of them and parents do nothing to stop it. I do not blame dogs for responding in this way, since it is a part of their natural behavior. Hugging dogs, lying on top of them, pinning them, or excessive handling makes dogs feel the need to break free. Bearing this in mind, there are several things that I will look for in the handling test.

Step 1. I start with the dog on the noose and offer him a treat. I will touch him gently on the head and move my way down the body. I touch the back, sides and underside of the dog. I will apply slight pressure to the front shoulders and back hips. I will stroke his tail and I may hold it for a brief moment. All of this is done while I maintain control of the rope attached to the dog's neck. It is important that there be enough slack in the rope to keep the dog from feeling tension, but the slack should be short enough to allow the handler to gain immediate control of the dog if he turns to bite. If he does turn to bite, our reaction should be indifferent.

We can correct the dog and protect ourselves, but getting emotional or angry is not part of our job on this test. If we see that the issue is fear-based, we can spend some time reassuring the dog and repeating the touch test to the sensitive area(s).

Most items covered here will elicit a unique response in different dogs. A dog that does not like to be touched can still be a good pet, but probably should not be placed with small children. Dogs that have hindquarter sensitivity or tail-handling issues also are not a good fit for children.

Again, the goal of a proper behavioral assessment is to clearly define the best home for a dog. By giving a dog a grade, we offer him a chance and open up space for other dogs.

Step 2. When testing the *touch phase*, I will also approach the dog from the rear, as some dogs spook easily when people do this. Some dogs will just turn around with surprise and then recover. The key to this is that the tester must remain neutral. If the tester spooks at the *dog's reaction*, the dog may nip or move forward, and rightfully so. Approaching a dog and then regressing elicits a forward motion from the dog (prey drive). If you approach the average dog and then regress, you will find that the dog moves forward. Similarly moving forward (as in chasing the dog) generally elicits a recoiling movement from the dog.

Step 3. During the touch phase, if I see a neutral or playful reaction from the dog I will continue on with the test. Next, I try to lift the dog's front paws and hold them for a brief moment. Slight pressure will show if there is any sensitivity in the dog's paws, which might require medical attention. I will also reward each touch with a reward, namely a treat. I want to remain fair to the dog and when a dog sees he's getting rewarded, he will more than likely go along with the test and not become irritated. There is no logic to testing a dog's limit unless you want the dog to fail. People who continue with a barrage of assaults on the dog, including pokes, jabs and overt handling are forcing a dog to fail. The test must remain neutral, and keeping the dog calm is the simplest way to keep the test neutral for the dog. If a dog responds positively when I act positively, I know his personality. Similarly, if a dog reacts negatively to me when I approach positively, I can be clear that there may be a problem.

Step 4. I will move along and see if the dog allows all of his paws and legs to be handled. If so, I continue. Remember, that a dog who offers his front legs is showing submission, rear legs have no indication of submission and are often more likely to elicit a different response. However, a dog that allows you to pick up all of his paws is generally a very solid dog, with few issues. This is rare, but there are dogs like this.

Step 5. With smaller dogs, I will try lifting them off of the ground to see how they respond to handling. Although I feel that carrying a dog is wrong unless it is injured, I do include it in my test because so many people insist on carrying smaller dogs. A dog should remain relaxed when I pick him up. Dogs that become stiff are not comfortable being picked up and should not be pushed any further.

Step 6. Although I am vehemently against pulling a dog's tail, I include it in my test because of the irresponsible parents who may not tell their child that this is wrong. Some dogs have a big issue with it. I watch the dog's head carefully as I grab hold of the tail and tug slightly. If the dog turns to bite, a good hold on his tail can protect you from getting bitten. However, you should still have hold of the leash with your other hand.

Step 7. Ears and eyes. To test a dog's ears and eyes, I squat next to the dog and rub his head and move over to the ears, lifting them up and gently massage them. I bring my hand forward toward the dog's nose and cover one eye at a time to see the dog's reaction. Ideally, the dog will not respond. A common response is for the dog to squirm his head around to move out from under your hand. If the dog does this more than once, he is not comfortable with eye handling and that should be noted. It is not a negative in any manner, unless the dog becomes aggressive or reactive.

Step 8. Mouth. I will rub the dog's head and move my hand toward his mouth. If he's fine, I can use my fingers to open the dog's lips and immediately offer him a treat. I'll repeat this on both sides. A dog that allows you to handle his mouth is another very rare candidate and getting this info will give us a stronger indication of a dog's limits. It's important to be extremely careful when handling a dog's mouth with your hands. I suggest watching for any indications, and if they arise, abort this portion of the test. There is no sense in getting bitten to prove a point.

As you may note, I offer a treat to a dog for compliance. This is important for the dog to see that he is being tested and not bribed. If he is truly a problem dog, he will respond negatively, whether I offer him a treat or not. Offering him a reward gives us a fair idea of his compliance. Those who argue that giving treats during a test sways the results are biased toward failing dogs in these tests.

Food test: Perhaps the worst aspect of temperament testing that has ever been introduced is the use of a plastic hand to test a dog for food aggression. I could write a book on this topic alone, but I'll withhold my litany and just say that it is idiotic for many reasons. The primary reason is that a dog that is eating should not be disturbed. For those people who think that this "test" is important because children may approach a dog while he is eating, I suggest that you train children not to interfere with a dog that is eating. Furthermore, a dog that bites a plastic hand is biting an object that has absolutely no relation to a human hand; he may or may not bite a hand, but the plastic one gives us no clear indication. You can use a broomstick or pipe with the exact same results.

Since dogs are creatures of scent, we are betraying the dog's strongest drive by introducing a plastic prosthetic because – whether it looks like a hand or not – it's not a human hand to the dog. Remember, there is no need to reach into a dog's bowl while he is eating – NONE! Dogs that have food issues may have a right to have these issues: if a dog has been at the shelter and has not had enough to eat or has lived in the streets where food is in short supply, he may exhibit behaviors that he has learned to keep him alive. I am more interested in a dog's food issues as they relate to other dogs, as opposed to humans. Furthermore, retraining a dog to lose biting tendencies toward people (not children) is not impossible. Therefore, with a little work we can fix a problem that would otherwise be a death sentence for a dog.

I test a dog for food issues using my hands and treats in a much different and much fairer way. I offer the dog a treat and let him take it from my hand. Then I offer another and partially remove it. I want to see the dog's drive in trying to get the treat back. Will he back down or pursue my hand for the treat? I want to see how the dog takes the treat from my hand. This will show me that the dog can differentiate my hand from a treat, and it also reveals his level of drive for food. I watch a dog's behavior when I have food in my hand, as well as when I reach into my bag or pouch for more food. I may even eat in front of the dog and watch his drive.

Follow these steps in order, and do not progress to the next step if the dog is reacting adversely in the current step.

Step 1. When the dog approaches, offer him a treat, preferably something about 3-6 inches long, such as a strip of jerky. Allow the dog to bite it off or break it off when it is in his mouth.

Step 2. Offer the dog another treat and, as he begins to bite down, pull the treat back out of his mouth. What is his reaction? Confusion? Regression? Assertiveness?

Step 3. Drop a piece of the treat on the ground and as soon as the dog sees it, cover it with your foot. Observe the reaction: Confusion? (Looking up to you.) Assertiveness? (Digging at the treat.) Indifference? (*Hopefully you are wearing boots.*)

Step 4. When the dog is eating the treat, begin some mild general handling (head patting, body contact, moving around). If he's steady and comfortable with you, he will continue eating the treat from your hand. If he gets confused, he will stop and back up. If he becomes irritated, he may growl or snap your hand.

Step 5. Initiate some mouth handling while the dog is eating the treat. I begin touching lips, chin, and nose and cover his eyes. These are trigger areas, but we are approaching them in a manner that is fair to the dog. The best result to see is a dog that remains focused on the food and pays little attention to your handling. Remember, you will not proceed to this step if the dog showed any adverse reaction in the previous step(s).

Step 6. Introduce another dog into the immediate (but not reachable) vicinity of the dog. Begin offering the other dog treats while the *test dog* is ignored. He should be close enough to see the other dog being fed, but not close enough to connect. At this point, if the dog has shown favorable responses to the rest of this test I move forward and bring the two dogs closer together. I will drop some treats for one dog, and immediately reach across and drop some for the other dog. I generally will do this with an assistant or I will tie one dog off to a pole. It will be nearly impossible to handle both dogs during this test and dispense food and watch for behaviors. Be diligent in this test – it will be an important part of the evaluation.

If your dog moves toward the other dog in a dominant manner, he should be corrected and reintroduced immediately.

By *dominant* it is understood that the dog is going after the other dog and not the food, and he is going after the other dog in order to get the food. The dogs should be able to take treats at the same time from the ground or should ignore the treats while the other dog eats. Both of these are highly favorable responses.

The correction here should be in the form of a leash correction, showing the dog that this behavior is not acceptable. To simply disqualify the dog for showing some food dominance is highly unfair. Once corrected, I've found that most dogs will settle down and share the treats or ignore the other dog. A dog that shows possessiveness toward food can be retrained, or an easier solution to the problem is to insist on a separate feeding area for the dog. Dogs in shelters are often very food possessive. This is in no way a red-strike against the dog; it is merely an observation toward better understanding of how to handle this particular dog.

Correction test: How a dog responds to basic corrections on a leash is a good indication of how well he will be able to adjust to many social environments.

Using the noose that we've left on the dog during the entire test, I will walk the dog around the field, near other people and near distractions. I will let the dog sniff something for a few moments and then give a slight tug on the leash followed, by a verbal direction. Here I look for his immediate and secondary responses.

Upon administering the correction, I look to see if he redirects his attention to me, which is what I'm looking for. Does he drop in fear, does his tail go between his legs or does his back become hunched? Does he completely ignore me and keep doing what he's doing? Or does he redirect toward me? That is to say, does he turn to bite the person who delivered the correction? Any reaction but the last one is okay. A dog that redirects and tries to bite the person delivering a slight redirection should be looked at further.

It is important that the correction be a tug on the leash, not a crushing blow. It will need to be scaled from smaller dogs to larger dogs and should be at the level to merely get the dog's attention away from what he is focused on. The rarest of dogs (I'd say less than 1 in 500) will redirect and try to bite the handler.

Dominance test: I want to be clear here that I suggest testing a dog for dominance without drawing a conclusion that a dominant dog is a bad dog. All dogs have a level of dominance and testing for *it* is paramount to understanding the dog. As a tester, I consider it my obligation to know what the dog will and will not tolerate. For example, if I am testing a dog that will be handled by children, I will grab the dog's tail and give it a slight tug. Yes, this may be a silly test, but I know for a fact that a child will pull a dog's tail given the chance, and if the parents are too ignorant to teach a child not to, I want to know what the dog's reaction will be. If the dog gets crazy from a tail pulling, I would note that and would not place the dog with small children.

Again, these tests are not to disqualify a dog from "passing or failing," simply to disqualify the dog from a home that would be unsuitable for the dog. Often times I will test a dog to see *when* he bites instead of *if* he bites. When I can find the threshold of the dog, I feel I know the dog. This isn't something I suggest for everyone, but for people with intensive experience it is a good tool.

If you're clear that the dog is dominant, it

is a bad idea to do the following tests, as you may get bitten. These tests are to classify a dog as dominant if we are uncertain, and if he displays dominant tendencies during the test, what will be his reaction? Will he move away to avoid or will he strike back?

Step 1. Push down on a dog's shoulders using your hand and forearm. Submissive dogs will melt down under slight pressure or slide away. A dominant dog will rear up or remain still and motionless in a way to communicate that he is about to attack.

Step 2. Directly stare at the dog's eyes. This is a test that sets off a dog's trigger, but because people do it, we test for it. Many dogs will look away or will engage with play barking. The dogs that get very still and begin snarling are the trigger we're looking to classify.

Step 3. Reach underneath a dog's backside. To do this, I start on the back leg and move up toward the inside of the thigh. We covered this in the previous handling section, but I want to re-address it here because a dominant dog will not tolerate it. If a dog becomes fidgety when you move up the inside of his/her leg it is not a dominant dog. Dominant dogs become still or will immediately snap. Be certain that the dog you are testing is secured and you are able to quickly move away. It is probably best to do this with a savvy dog handler helping you.

Step 4. Remove a toy from a dog's proximity or mouth. Again, another topic that I covered previously, but I want to see the dog's reaction. If you are removing the item from the dog, I suggest you have the dog restrained in a manner that will limit his mobility as you reach in. A better way, depending if one is available, is to use a helper who will be able to pull the dog back and away from you if the dog strikes. Be certain that the person has keen reflexes and the strength to keep the dog from getting to you.

Closed environment test: This section can be done at the beginning or end of the test. I generally use the kennel for this or a corner of the field. I want to see how the dog responds to small areas or confinement. I don't advise this test with dogs that have already displayed territorial issues.

The first thing I look for is how the dog will respond to my approaching him when he is in a corner. Many dogs will dart out and go to another area of the kennel. Others will become very submissive. Still others will posture and make it known that they will attack.

To handle this in a fair manner, it is important to be neutral on the approach and not directly confront the dog – in particular a dog that is already showing signs of adverse behavior to the environment. If you *storm* the area and the dog reacts and then label the dog as territorially aggressive, it's a highly unfair assessment. We want to see if the dog is truly exhibiting issues about the environment first, and not about our approach to it.

In order to achieve this, we offer the dog a small treat, usually thrown to them. We do not engage in verbal interaction with the dog. If the dog takes the treat and his body language becomes more open, we continue. After a few moments, we approach closer and closer to see at which point the dog becomes responsive to our encroachment. If the dog never becomes open and continues to posture in a fearful or dominant manner, we will try to move the dog to another area of confinement to see if the behavior is specific to his current environment or the overall concept of confinement.

If he is only reactive to his personal environment, we will need to spend some time working him on territorial issues. If it is every area, it is generally an issue of fear, which can be addressed through basic structure training. Dogs that outright attack when you approach their areas are the ones of great concern. This response is generally seen in dogs that were previously *chained.* Retraining *this* is possible, but a bit of work, depending on their level of aggression.

Loud noise / startle response: Loud noises can illicit several reactions in dogs: neutrality, assertion, curiosity or withdrawal. If a dog is easily spooked by loud noises, he may be fearful and may react adversely in stimulating environments. This can include a car backfiring, thunder, slamming doors, dropping an item on the floor, loud music, etc. Also, dogs that become fearful or reactive to loud noises may become spooked. We do not worry if a dog responds through withdrawal: instead we are looking for a heavily skewed reaction such as growling or immediate posturing. A dog may get spooked by a loud noise and pull away, then immediately return in a curious manner. This is a very positive sign.

Many dogs that are used for police work, bite sports; SAR, etc., are generally acclimated to loud noises at an early age. It is important that these types of dogs are neutral to loud sounds because they will encounter them on a regular basis. One of the most desired responses is a reaction to the initial sound and then a curious, investigative follow up.

To test a dog for this, I do the following:

- When the dog is focused on a toy or a treat, I drop a metal bowl about 2-3 feet away from its head on a cement floor. If there is only grass, I use two bowls and clang them together.

- Slam a kennel door as the dog walks out or walks by.

- As the dog is walking through the kennel, I'll knock something over as he walks by. This can be a broom, a wet floor sign or anything.

- When the dog is focused on someone or something in the testing area a loud clap about 2-3 feet behind his head.

It is important that the dog not recognize that the sounds are related to you. When the dog turns toward you, the object (for example, the bowl you dropped) should be out of your hands. If you clanged two bowls together, move them behind your back immediately after making the noise.

This test can be repeated a few times with different items and different locations. It is important to note that the *noise test* is looking for what is called a *startle response.* All too often, people test dogs for startle response by throwing something at the dog. This is incorrect because it is a direct threat to the dog. The dog should not feel any threat by the item. That is why it is best to have the sound "just happen."

If we see a sharp (or negative) response from the dog, we can move along in the test and add another startle test a little later on. On the subsequent noises, the dog should become more accustomed to the sounds and react with less and less surprise.

It is important to remember that there is no failing on this section of the test because the dog becomes fearful or jolted by the response. The only negative response is a dog that will turn toward aggression when startled by a sound.

Some people test a dog's startle response by poking him when he's not looking. I find this to be an unnecessary test unless the dog is going to a home with uncontrollable small children, which I don't believe is a suitable home for any dog. It is as unfair as running up behind you and smacking you and seeing what your response is. Behavioral assessment tests must, above all, be fair.

Other dogs: Introducing dogs to other dogs is a science in and of itself. Just because a dog reacts negatively to another dog through a cage or fence is no indication that the dog will show this same reaction when the barrier is removed. Also, some dogs display aggression toward other dogs when they themselves are on a leash but will not act aggressively when in a free environment. These indications are generally due to improper socialization and are important things to note during our test. It is not a good idea to simply take two dogs and put them together in a yard to put this concept to the test. We strive to introduce two dogs in a fair manner and see their personality.

We should start by understanding that certain dogs will respond in certain ways. Dominant dogs will posture and assume a position. Male to female interaction can elicit a sexual posture. My position is generally to introduce like- sex dogs for basic temperament testing. The reason for this is, that like-sex fights tend to be the most common and most problematic.

A crucial aspect of the dog-to-dog test is that the dog we are testing our candidate against should be neutral. If the other dog is high-strung, overly fearful, dominant or very reactive, the test is highly unfair. A good testing dog is hard to find, and once found is worth his weight in gold.

I start the test through the fence and always make sure that the person handling the other dog in the yard is competent and able to understand my directions. I also want a person who will follow my direction at a moment's notice and not stall, which could cause serious injury to both dog and tester.

I will walk through the gate and into the yard, and then go my way while my assistant holds her dog on a stay. I watch my dog for any indication of curiosity. I walk my dog by the other dog a couple of times, and if the other dog is a good helper (not lunging, growling, barking or acting up), I will allow my dog to go over and greet him. I do not let them meet if either or both of them are too excited. I keep my leash loose and ask my assistant to do the same with hers. Again, I only allow this if I see that the dogs are neutral. If they are not, I will walk away and reintroduce. I do not introduce two dogs that are high-strung. The sniffing or introduction lasts only a few moments (a count of 3-5 is often enough). Then I remove my dog or have my assistant remove hers.

When I say *remove* the dog, I do NOT yank them away from each other, as this can create a negative response or experience. This response will be a direct response to the way the dog was removed, *not* a response to the other dog. If all goes well, I will go back over and reintroduce, then move the dogs apart and stroke the other dog's head. I'm looking for a reaction in my dog. I'm looking for neutrality. I will take this as far as feeding them both treats when they are sitting close to each other. I do, however, always assure that I have enough time and space to pull the dogs apart in the event that they become territorial or aggressive. If it is necessary to separate two dogs that are becoming aggressive, it should be done in a firm yet unemotional manner. There should be no yelling or explaining. The dogs are separated and reintroduced.

I've performed tests in which I had to reintroduce two dogs 4 to 5 times before they understood that they should get along. In these situations I can put a note on the dog's file that the dog *can* be fine with other dogs if he is introduced properly. There are certain dogs that – even with proper introduction – cannot get along with another dog. Again, this should be noted. Most dogs have no issues with other dogs, if properly introduced. The shelter environment is not the best place to properly introduce two dogs if they have issues.

The most important thing to watch for in dog-to-dog testing is that the leashes don't get tangled. If they do, you have a major issue. Pulling on tangled leashes is a certain way to get two dogs to engage.

Reaching in to separate them while the dogs are engaged is a certain way to get bit. If, during a test the leashes get tangled, I will drop my leash, grab a toy or treat and call my dog to me at the same time I ask my assistant to stand still. The faster I can back away, the faster the dog will try to follow. I would suggest that you be extremely careful to avoid leash tangles in the first place during a test, and if they happen, react quickly, with no panic.

Continuing on with the test, I approach the test dog from the side while he is involved with the other dog. I will touch him and see his reaction. I will poke him gently and see if he will redirect to me; I want to see if he is locked in on the other dog or if his primary focus will come back to me. Some dogs are so focused on other dogs that they prefer the other dogs to their handler. I want to see if I can redirect the dog back to me while he is engaged with the other dog. This is not a pass or fail aspect, but it's a bonus for a dog to prefer the company of his handler to that of the other dog. Don't get your feelings hurt if only one in a hundred dogs redirects to you. Dogs generally prefer the company of other dogs to humans.

After performing these segments – presuming all went well – I will take both dogs with me and walk around the field. I will keep them separated (one on each side of me) and walk around the field and watch their reaction. You should have adequate control of the leashes in the event they cross in front of or behind you. They should be immediately separated and you should continue the walk. It is the rarest of exceptions that will allow me to have both dogs walk on the same side. I can get a good enough indication of the dog's temperament toward each other while walking with them on either side of me.

If the test dog does fine on all aspects of these tests, there is a strong indication that he will have no issues with any dog that he will meet. It's important to note that dogs may respond differently to unfamiliar handlers. If someone is very skittish of two dogs meeting, they may trigger a response in the dog that is negative and the dog may react differently than he did in our test.

Conclusion: As a tester, it is our goal to be as fair to the dog we are testing as possible. We should understand that our evaluation is not only important to the dog we test, but also to the other dogs that this dog will encounter, as well as to the humans he will meet. We want to give every dog a fair shot at a good life and we don't want to surprise any new dog owners with a situation they are unaware or unable to control.

This test is not designed to rule out a dog from potential adoption, but rather to make educated suggestions as to the best home for a particular dog. Also, dogs that display behavioral problems during a test should be made available to animal rescue organizations so that they may rehabilitate them and place them afterwards.

I don't believe in pass or fail tests if there are rescue organizations available to take dogs that have some behavioral issues. That is why rescue exists!

By drawing some conclusions and gaining a better understanding of dogs before adopting them out, we open the doors to helping more dogs get into better homes. We also lessen the likelihood that dogs will be returned for behavioral issues. The easier we make the placement of easily adoptable dogs, the more time we can spend focused on helping the dogs that need to be rescued.

I also suggest that if people are considering adopting a dog into a home that already has a dog, they should bring their dog to meet the new candidate. This can save a lot of work, aggravation and heartache by watching their initial interaction. Introducing the dog into the home is something that should be done with time, but it is a good idea to see how two dogs will interact upon first meeting. The potential owners should be made to sign a release form to hold harmless the shelter, staff, management, etc., and the family's dog should be current on all vaccinations. If a face-to-face meeting cannot be arranged, it's a good idea to see their interaction through a gate or fence.

This is not a make-or-break introduction, but rather a basic test to see initial reactions. When introducing a new dog into a home, I suggest reading and sharing the article on www.boundangels.org entitled "***Bringing Home the New Dog***."

Closing thoughts: Testing a dog's behavior is a talent that is more feeling than technical. I feel that people can learn this skill to some degree, but there are those who are *naturals*. It is always best to have someone who has a natural gift to act as the tester whenever possible. This guide is designed to help people of any level to better understand canine behavior. All staff, volunteers and management who have interaction with dogs should read it, whether or not they are performing the test.

As I mentioned previously, there is an inherent risk of injury in any interaction with any dog. I strongly urge you to take caution. Caution is better than valor – and when in doubt, get **out**. Be smart about your decisions and your opinions when testing a dog. There are certain dogs that can be rehabilitated and some that cannot. I believe that those dogs that can't be helped are the smallest percentage, but they do exist. It is my goal with this book to open your eyes to better help those that can be saved, and save them.

join the revolution!

Robert Cabral
Bound Angels / Black Belt Dog Training

www.boundangels.org

CPSIA information can be obtained
at www.ICGtesting.com
Printed in the USA
LVHW040855060319
609683LV00001B/39

9 780985 741310